Issues in Contemporary Diplomacy (II): Diplomacy and Human Rights

Building Bridges in a Changing World

Hichem Karoui, Foreword by Dr Abdulaziz Al-Hurr

Global East-West (London) The Diplomatic Institute (Doha)

Copyright © 2025 by Hichem Karoui

Series: Issues in Contemporary Diplomacy

I. The Art of Diplomacy: Its Development and Modern Forms.

II. Diplomacy and human rights: building bridges in a changing world.

III. Track II diplomacy: informal paths to peace.

Collection : Diplomacy

Global East-West (London).

All rights reserved.

No portion of this book may be reproduced in any form without written permission from the publisher or author, except as permitted by copyright law.

Contents

Acknowledgements	1
Foreword	5
By His Excellency Ambassador Dr Abdulaziz bin Mohammed Al-Hurr	
1. Introduction	15
Diplomacy and Human Rights in the New World Order	
2. History of Diplomacy	29
From Ancient Times to the Modern Era	
References	39
3. Human Rights Origins and Development	45
In International Community	
References	59
4. The Relationship Between Diplomacy and Human Rights	65
Interactions and Challenges	
References	81

5. Diplomacy as a Tool for Defending Human Rights	87
References	101
6. International Organisations And the Shaping of Human Rights Standards	105
References	119
7. Current Challenges Facing Human Rights Diplomats	125
References	139
8. National Sovereignty Versus Human Rights An Impossible Balance?	143
References	157
9. Human Rights Economics The Mutual Impact of Economics and Rights	161
References	177
10. Effective Diplomacy Strategies for Promoting Human Rights	183
References	197
11. Technology and Human Rights Future Opportunities for Advancing Rights	203
References	217

12. Conclusion 223
   Towards Diplomacy Based on Awareness and Responsibility

Acknowledgements

I am profoundly grateful to the many individuals and institutions whose support, encouragement, and expertise have made this research endeavour possible. The publication of "Issues in Contemporary Diplomacy" represents not merely an academic exercise, but a collaborative effort that has benefited immeasurably from the generosity and vision of those who believed in its importance.

First and foremost, I extend my deepest appreciation to His Excellency Ambassador Dr Abdulaziz bin Mohammed Al-Hurr, Director of the Diplomatic Institute at the Ministry of Foreign Affairs of Qatar. His immediate and unwavering support when I first proposed this project was both inspiring and enabling. Without his encouragement to complete this work and his commitment to seeing it through to publication, this endeavour would not have come to fruition. His leadership and dedication to advancing diplomatic scholarship exemplify the highest standards of intellectual patronage.

I am equally indebted to the Presidential apparatus of the Ministry of Foreign Affairs of Qatar for graciously granting approval for this work to be undertaken as one of the research projects of the Diplomatic Institute. This institutional backing has been invaluable in providing both the framework and the credibility necessary for a project of this scope and ambition.

My sincere gratitude extends to Dr Nawzad Abdurrahman Al Hiti, whose invaluable assistance in facilitating communications and information exchange throughout the production of this book has been instrumental to its completion. His scholarly insights and practical support have enriched this work immeasurably.

I also wish to acknowledge the dedicated staff of the Diplomatic Institute and the Ministry of Foreign Affairs who have been involved in the production of this work. Their professionalism, attention to detail, and commitment to excellence have ensured that this publication meets the highest standards befitting such an important institution.

The simultaneous publication of this work in Arabic, English, and French reflects the universal relevance of diplomatic studies and the commitment to making this research accessible to scholars and practitioners across linguistic and cultural boundaries. This achievement would not have been possible without the collective effort of all those mentioned above.

Finally, I acknowledge that whilst this first volume marks the beginning of what, I hope, will be a significant contribution to contemporary diplomatic scholarship, it represents the culmination of countless hours of support, guidance, and encouragement from the Qatari diplomatic community. It is my sincere hope that this work will serve to advance our understanding of the complex challenges and opportunities facing diplomacy in the modern world.

Hichem Karoui

Foreword

By His Excellency Ambassador Dr Abdulaziz bin Mohammed Al-Hurr

This trilogy contains three comprehensive studies, all related to diplomacy. Since its establishment, the Diplomatic Institute has been publishing research, studies, reports and various publications that contribute to its training programmes and support its core mission of preparing, qualifying and training Ministry of Foreign Affairs employees to work in the diplomatic and consular corps and in the field of international cooperation. We have a special department at the Institute that prepares studies and research in collaboration with our experts and academics. Our goal is to ensure that trainees and postgraduate students in diplomacy and international relations find, within the Diplomatic Institute's publications and its library, what they need to study and understand before joining their jobs and while performing their duties, whenever they need it.

At this institute, we seek to establish a special library that focuses on the subjects covered by our training and study programmes. In this context, we will work, God willing, in cooperation with experts in the field, to publish more books and publications of intellectual value and relevance to our interests, so that they may benefit Ministry of Foreign Affairs employees and those invited to participate in our training courses in various programmes, from 'Foundations' to 'Capabilities' and even the 'Executive Master's' programme for distinguished diplomats.

This work is another addition to a series of valuable

publications in the same field. It is divided into three volumes, as follows:
  I. The Art of Diplomacy: Its Development and Modern Forms.
  II. Diplomacy and human rights: building bridges in a changing world.
  III. Track II diplomacy: informal paths to peace.

The first volume examines the development of diplomacy throughout history. It reviews the historical roots of diplomacy, tracing its evolution from ancient civilisations through the Middle Ages, the European Renaissance, and the era of expansion and empires following the Great Industrial Revolution, as well as the transformations, conflicts, and wars of the 20th century that have influenced and shaped diplomacy into its current form. This volume also delves into the historical frameworks, concepts and protocols specific to each era and each form of diplomacy, including traditional diplomacy, public diplomacy, economic diplomacy, cultural diplomacy, digital diplomacy, environmental diplomacy, multilateral diplomacy, and new players in the diplomatic field, such as non-governmental organisations and multinational corporations, among other related topics. It is a comprehensive introduction to the subject.

The second volume analyses the relationship between diplomacy and human rights in the modern world, examines the development of diplomacy and the understanding of human rights throughout history, and discusses the interactions between them and the challenges they face. It also details the role of international organisations and analyses the relationship between national sovereignty and human rights. Similarly, it discusses the economy and technology in relation to human rights, as well as other issues of great importance that diplomats must be aware of.

The third and final volume of this trilogy is devoted to examining a form of diplomatic work that is unfamiliar to many, perhaps because it is difficult for the media to follow. It essentially shuns the limelight, preferring to work behind the scenes, considering this one of the conditions for success in its tasks. This, of course, refers to track II diplomacy. This last volume provides a comprehensive and detailed analysis of the development of this type of diplomacy, comparing it with first-track diplomacy and highlighting the differences, benefits, roles and mechanisms of action. It traces the evolution of Track II from the classical era to the digital age, highlighting the distinctions and synergies between the two tracks and providing models, examples and analysis of strategies, methodologies and political and social contexts. It also reviews the elements that contribute to a greater or lesser extent to the distinction and success of second-track diplomacy whenever the first track fails, through case studies and lessons learnt.

The analysis concludes with recommendations for addressing contemporary global issues.

As this brief overview shows, the trilogy we are presenting to you today addresses topics that are still being discussed everywhere in the field of diplomacy. It begins with a definition of diplomacy and its historical development, devoting a whole volume to this topic. Familiarity with this aspect is essential for anyone who aspires to work in the Foreign Ministry and climb the diplomatic ladder. Every diplomat must at least know the history of their profession, its forms and its developments.

Devoting another volume to the study of the relationship between diplomacy and human rights is justified, especially since we, in Qatar, consider this issue to be fundamental to our foreign policy. Perhaps the most prominent example we can mention in this regard is the Palestinian issue, which is currently the most pressing human rights issue. It is an issue that is always present in Qatar's official and popular diplomacy, as well as in its Track II Diplomacy, which will be discussed in the third volume of this work.

At every annual session of the United Nations General Assembly, His Highness Sheikh Tamim bin Hamad Al Thani, may God protect him, stands before the representatives of the world's nations and peoples at the UN podium, reminding them of the injustice inflicted on the Palestinian people since the first half of the last century, calling for the restoration of rights to their rightful owners, an end to the killing of innocent people and the displacement of millions from their ancestral lands, and rejecting the claim that 'Israel has the right to defend itself.'

The importance of this fundamental human rights

issue is evident from the fact that His Highness the Emir devoted half of his speech at the 79th session of the General Assembly to defending it and discussing Qatar's role in mediating a ceasefire and a return to negotiations for a just solution to the Palestinian issue. As a reminder, His Highness said, for example:

> "What the Palestinian people in the Gaza Strip are experiencing today is the most barbaric and horrific aggression and the most flagrant violation of human values and international conventions and norms. This is not a war in the sense of war as it is commonly understood and used in international relations, but rather a crime of genocide using the latest weapons against a people trapped in a prison camp with no escape from the barrage of bombs dropped by aircraft. Resolutions, condemnations and reports have been exhausted, and all that remains is the naked, premeditated and unrestrained crime, whose victims are children, women and the elderly."

To emphasise that the issue seems to be that the world's major powers are not concerned with the Palestinian human rights that Israel violates on a daily basis, despite the provisions of UN regulations, resolutions and recommendations, and even the constitutions and laws of those nations themselves, His Highness Sheikh Tamim, may God protect him, said in the same speech:

> "Every year, I stand on this podium and begin my speech by talking about the Palestinian issue, the absence of justice, the dangers of believing that it can be ignored, and the illusions of peace without a just solution. I have done so every year at a time when the Palestinian issue has been absent from the speeches of representatives of major powers in our world (...)."

His Highness added:

> "The Israeli aggression that has been ongoing for nearly a year is nothing but the result of a lack of sincere political will, deliberate international inaction to resolve the Palestinian issue fairly, and the insistence of the Israeli occupying authorities on imposing a fait accompli on the Palestinians and the world by all means of force. The ongoing brutal war has dealt a fatal blow to international legitimacy and severely damaged the credibility of the concepts on which the international community was founded after the Second World

War."

Is there any statement more telling than that of His Highness, may God protect him, which places the issue of Palestinian human rights at the forefront of Qatari diplomacy?

In the third volume of this work, we find an overview of second-track diplomacy, which anyone who aspires to succeed in diplomatic missions must understand well, especially since Qatar now has considerable experience in mediating for peace and negotiating complex issues between parties that find it difficult to meet directly at the negotiating table. This makes the second track the only way to resolve any issue that has reached an impasse. This applies to various cases in which Qatar has contributed to the success of negotiations away from the spotlight.

Without further ado, we hope that this work will be of benefit to Ministry of Foreign Affairs staff and trainees at the Diplomatic Institute in the first place, as well as to postgraduate students of diplomacy and international relations.

> {And say: **Work; so Allah will see your work and (so will) His Messenger and the believers**}

Ambassador Dr Abdulaziz Mohammed Al-Hurr, Director of the Diplomatic Institute (Ministry of Foreign Affairs), Qatar.

1
Introduction

Diplomacy and Human Rights in the New World Order

Definition of Diplomacy and Human Rights

The concepts of diplomacy and human rights form an essential core of international interaction, with diplomacy being a set of policies and techniques used to interact with other political systems to achieve national interests. On the other hand, human rights are concerned with the protection and guarantee of the fundamental rights and individual freedoms of individuals without discrimination. These two broad fields interact with each other in a simultaneous and interrelated manner in the context of global developments. In the context of recent global developments, it appears that diplomacy has responded to the new challenges posed by the rapid development of globalisation and technology. In this context, it is necessary to consider how this development affects diplomacy and human rights in international communities.

The nature of relations between states and international communities has changed with shifts in international politics and global powers. The question now is how the practice of diplomacy can promote human rights in this complex context. Therefore, it is important to thoroughly understand the interactive influence of diplomacy on human rights within the new world order to assess how diplomacy can serve as a tool for promoting human rights. This issue will remain our primary focus throughout the chapters of this book to understand the depth of the relationship between diplomacy and human rights and how this relationship affects international practice.

Global development and its impact on diplomacy

Global development is one of the most influential factors in the field of diplomacy, as international relations have undergone radical transformations as a result of political, economic and social developments at the global level. This is evident in the nature of modern international relations and how diplomacy interacts with these transformations. The advancement of globalisation and technology, as well as changes in the international system, have made diplomatic engagement more complex and challenging.

The new international system is witnessing growing conflicts and challenges that require diplomatic strategies different from those that were customary in the past. Such an evolution has led to changes in diplomatic priorities and in the form of cooperation between states. In addition, global economic shifts and a growing interest in sustainable development have added a new dimension to the current dynamics of diplomacy. It is important to understand the impact of these shifts on the role of diplomacy and those seeking to achieve global stability and human rights. Continuous global development requires research and a profound understanding of its causes and effects to ensure that diplomacy responds effectively to contemporary challenges and formulates policies that enhance its role in achieving global stability and peace.

The Place of Human Rights in Modern International Politics

In today's world, human rights are a vital part of international politics. People view the respect and promotion of human rights as essential for the stability of international systems and relations. Modern international politics reflects a commitment to promoting the fundamental rights of individuals, both within national borders and across them.

Human rights organisations and international human rights treaties represent key bases for shaping international policy and guiding international relations. This emphasis on human rights is evident in numerous international agreements, such as the Universal Declaration of Human Rights and the United Nations Convention against Torture, among others. Commitment to human rights forms the basis for building international relations based on mutual respect and justice.

Thus, the place of human rights in modern international politics reflects a trend toward recognising the importance of human rights as a global issue that transcends national borders and influences international interactions in various ways. With continued advances in communication technology and the widespread dissemination of information, these international policies on human rights are becoming more influential and important in building a more equitable and peaceful world.

Diplomacy in the Face of New Global Challenges

In the international arena, diplomacy plays a crucial role in advancing national interests and bolstering relations between states. As the world evolves and new challenges emerge, the role of diplomats has become more complex and challenging. Today's world faces multiple challenges, including climate change, humanitarian crises, international conflicts, migration, and the spread of infectious diseases, as is the case with the COVID-19 pandemic. All these challenges call for effective and diverse diplomatic responses. Human rights issues occupy a central place in this context, as addressing them requires joint efforts and international understanding.

The diplomatic tools that can be used to address

these challenges vary, ranging from bilateral talks between states to public diplomacy activities and advocacy for international alliances. This situation requires harmony between foreign policy and diplomatic efforts to ensure that the interests of states are achieved while simultaneously promoting human rights. International institutions play an important role in this context, facilitating international cooperation and setting international human rights standards.

It is necessary to create new visions and adopt sophisticated diplomatic policies that are in tune with the new reality and build innovative solutions to meet the challenges of the times. Such an endeavour requires activating cooperation between states and enhancing their ability to adapt to global changes. Despite the complexities of these circumstances, contemporary diplomacy can facilitate balance and mediation, thereby promoting development and ensuring international peace. Thus, the role of diplomacy in the face of new global challenges emerges as a vital tool for achieving sustainable development and promoting human rights.

Diplomatic tools for promoting human rights

Diplomacy is one of the main tools for promoting and protecting human rights in the international community. To achieve tangible progress in the field of human rights, these tools encompass a variety of measures and policies. Among the most prominent diplomatic tools that can be used are negotiation and diplomatic mediation, where diplomats can use their negotiation skills to reach international agreements to protect and ensure respect for human rights.

In addition, diplomacy can be used as a means of monitoring and evaluating respect for human rights in countries and pressuring governments to take the necessary measures to improve the situation. Cultural diplomacy and cultural exchange can also contribute to raising awareness of human rights issues and promoting human values in societies.

Examples of diplomacy interacting with human rights

We can observe many examples and interactions that highlight the role of diplomacy in preserving and promoting human rights at the international level. The 2015 Paris Agreement on climate change is one notable example of international diplomatic efforts to achieve human rights, as the signatory states sought to limit the effects of climate change on the environment and, consequently, on human life and the right to live in a healthy environment. As we can see from the negotiations and diplomatic efforts made during that process, diplomatic interests played an important role in reaching international consensus on this issue. We can also see this in the way the world has responded to the coronavirus pandemic.

Health diplomacy has made it easier for countries to work together to fight the virus and deal with its humanitarian effects. We have witnessed the exchange of expertise and cooperation between countries in the field of medical research and the distribution of vaccines and medical resources, demonstrating the extent of diplomacy's impact on the realisation of human rights, especially in the context of healthcare emergencies.

When we examine local models, we also find them to be tangible, as agricultural diplomacy illustrates its role in supporting the rights of farmers and agricultural workers at both local and international government policy levels. Trade agreements and diplomatic negotiations can achieve a balance that protects the rights of workers and farmers while promoting general economic interests. These models and interactions show how diplomacy can be one of the effective tools in achieving human rights at the global and local levels, and highlight the importance of its positive interactions in achieving global humanitarian goals.

Contemporary Challenges to Diplomacy and Human Rights

The contemporary world faces many challenges that affect the role of diplomacy in protecting and promoting human rights. Among these challenges is the escalation of international conflicts and armed disputes, which jeopardise human rights and hinder diplomatic efforts to protect them. The world also faces increasing challenges in the field of human rights as a result of economic and social conditions, requiring intensified diplomatic efforts to address these new challenges.

The impact of environmental conditions and climate change on human rights is also a contemporary challenge that requires an effective diplomatic response. In addition, increasing social and cultural divisions and tensions in the modern world reinforce the importance of diplomacy in achieving understanding and cooperation between states and societies.

The challenges of trade agreements and the global economy also affect human rights, and diplomacy must ensure a balance between global trade and the preservation of human rights. These challenges form the basis for the need to review existing diplomatic methods and strategies to adapt to the contemporary global context and to maintain the protection and promotion of human rights in the face of these new challenges.

Multilateral diplomacy and its impact on human rights

'Multilateral diplomacy' is a term that refers to cooperation and interaction between several states or international entities to achieve common goals, often including the promotion of human rights and human stability. This type of diplomacy is of enormous importance in the modern world, where major global challenges are increasing, and it is becoming necessary for states and international organisations to work together to address these complex challenges and humanitarian crises. One of the most important aspects of multilateral diplomacy is its ability to address complex humanitarian issues, such as illegal migration, armed conflict, food security, and climate change.

Through cooperation and coordination between different parties, multilateral diplomacy can play an effective role in achieving comprehensive and sustainable solutions to these important humanitarian issues. In addition, multilateral diplomacy contributes to promoting dialogue and understanding between different cultures, which leads to the promotion of human rights values and cooperation between communities. This cultural and personal interaction can provide a platform for building bridges of understanding and international cooperation based on common interests and shared human values. With the development of technology and the international community's increasing awareness of the importance of human rights, it is important to acknowledge the role of multilateral diplomacy in promoting these values and achieving human stability. With joint efforts and effective cooperation, this type of diplomacy can have a significant impact on achieving noble humanitarian goals and shaping a better world for future generations.

Diplomatic Response to Humanitarian Crises

Humanitarian crises are among the most challenging issues facing the international community, including wars, armed conflicts, natural disasters, displacement, and extreme poverty. The whole world needs to act quickly and effectively in response to these crises. International diplomacy plays a vital role in addressing these crises and seeking sustainable solutions. The diplomatic response must be impartial and based on human rights principles, with a focus on mediation, negotiation, and finding solutions based on justice and equality.

All possible diplomatic channels, including bilateral communications and international organisations, should be used to ensure that crises do not escalate and that those affected receive necessary assistance.

This requires international cooperation and mutual support between states, as well as the exchange of information and expertise to achieve effective coordination.

Furthermore, all diplomatic responses to humanitarian crises should be studied and evaluated to develop future policies and procedures. Addressing humanitarian crises is a real challenge for international diplomacy and the promotion of human rights, and therefore the response must be comprehensive and integrated, reflecting states' commitment to human rights standards and humanitarian values.

Conclusion: Diplomacy as a fundamental means of achieving human rights

Establishing and realising human rights is one of the most important priorities in the world today, and in this context, diplomacy plays a crucial role in promoting and protecting these rights. Although diplomacy is often associated with international affairs and relations between states, it has also become an effective means of intervening in the protection of human rights.

Diplomacy can be a means of achieving balance between states and contributing to overcoming obstacles to the realisation of human rights. The formation of diplomatic agreements and treaties related to human rights can have a profound impact on their protection. Diplomatic talks and negotiations can also be a means of influencing states and motivating them to understand and respect human rights. Through sustained and intelligent diplomatic pressure, significant progress can be made in achieving justice and equality, as well as the protection of civil, political, economic, social, and cultural rights.

Furthermore, diplomacy can play an effective role in coordinating states and international organisations to provide humanitarian assistance in times of crisis, support communities in need, and improve their conditions. It is worth emphasising that diplomacy, if properly and strategically directed, can be a fundamental pillar for the realisation and protection of human rights in our new global order.

2
History of Diplomacy
From Ancient Times to the Modern Era

Ancient civilisations like the Egyptian, Indian, and Chinese are the origins of diplomacy. The ancient governments played a major role in establishing relations with each other, which led to the exchange of letters, envoys, and diplomatic negotiations. [1] Ancient civilisations are an important reference for understanding how diplomacy emerged as a science and an art, and how it evolved to become the diplomatic system we know today. [2]

Diplomacy in ancient civilisations

In ancient civilisations, relations between nations were conducted through what could be described as the earliest forms of diplomacy, with rulers and leaders exchanging envoys and letters to strengthen alliances or resolve disputes. For instance, certain figures in Ancient Egypt were responsible for communicating with other kingdoms and establishing trade and political relations. Diplomatic correspondence was also common in the Babylonian, Assyrian and Phoenician civilisations.[4]

In ancient India and China, these civilisations used diplomacy to negotiate trade and political agreements, as well as form military alliances. The famous Chinese thinker Confucius is considered one of the most influential figures in shaping the principles and foundations of diplomacy and international relations.[5] The development of these diplomatic methods in ancient civilisations indicates the importance of international relations and constructive dialogue since ancient times.[6]

Diplomatic systems in classical times

During classical times, diplomacy underwent remarkable developments and complex systems. During this period, multiple states emerged in regions such as the Middle East, India, and ancient Europe. Each state had its independent diplomatic system with its own rules and values. Diplomatic methods varied according to society and culture. The Greeks and Romans pioneered new techniques in diplomacy [7] that opened the door to international relations. [8]

In the Middle East, diplomacy flourished in civilisations such as the Pharaohs, Babylon and Assyria, where it enjoyed deep-rooted traditions and precise organisation. India also witnessed the development of diplomacy during the period of the warring states and beyond. The history of diplomacy during this period is interesting, given the great cultural and political diversity among different civilisations. The diplomatic transformations of the classical era marked a turning point in the history of international relations [9], as they contributed to the establishment of the foundations and rules on which diplomacy in later eras was based.

Diplomatic transformations during the Middle Ages

During the Middle Ages, diplomacy underwent radical shifts, stemming from changes in the political, cultural, and social systems of Europe and the Middle East. Wars and religious conflicts were among the main factors that influenced diplomatic practices during this period, as tensions between kingdoms and empires increased. Diplomacy during this period also saw the development of the use of diplomatic letters and communications between rulers and states to resolve disputes and conflicts.

New aspects of diplomacy also emerged during the Middle Ages, such as the role of mediators, ambassadors and international negotiators, leading to the development of diplomatic techniques and practices. [10] Eastern and Western cultures greatly influenced diplomatic practices in the Middle Ages, resulting in a diversity and richness of diplomatic texts and treaties. Diplomatic relations also saw developments in the use of diplomatic languages and cultural dialogues between rulers and governments. Despite the challenges and conflicts of the Middle Ages, diplomatic practices contributed to the development of international relations and communication among different civilisations.

The role of diplomacy in the Renaissance

The Renaissance witnessed major shifts in diplomacy and relations between states. It was a period of social, cultural, and intellectual change in Europe, where science, the arts, and literature flourished, and a new movement was launched aimed at opening channels of communication and contact between different countries. The role of diplomacy in the Renaissance was pivotal in establishing commercial and political relations between European and Eastern countries. Diplomatic practices were influenced by the intellectual and cultural developments that societies were experiencing at the time. [11]

Diplomacy in the Renaissance era was characterised by a regal and luxurious appearance, with major countries allocating their resources to developing diplomatic missions and building luxurious embassy palaces. Diplomacy during this period served to strengthen cultural and economic relations between countries, in addition to efforts to maintain the balance of political power.

Diplomacy in the Renaissance also witnessed a new momentum in the field of cultural relations and scientific exchange, with diplomatic missions emerging as centres for cultural communication and the transfer of knowledge between people. Diplomacy played a major role in the transfer of knowledge, arts and sciences between countries, which contributed to laying the foundations for cultural dialogue and human exchange.[12] Thus, the Renaissance was an important period in the history of diplomacy, as new ideas and social and cultural developments gave new impetus to diplomatic relations and laid the foundations for modern international interaction. [13]

Diplomatic protocols and practices in the biggest empires

In the era of powerful empires, diplomacy evolved and became a matter of precise protocol. Diplomatic protocols played a vital role in establishing stable and reliable international relations. Diplomatic practices during this period reflected the power and grandeur of the mighty empires. [14] These practices involved the use of embellishment, cheerfulness, and an emphasis on formal protocols and strict rules of diplomatic conduct. Feelings of desire to assert dominance and sovereignty prevailed through diplomatic protocols, formal ceremonies, and important diplomatic visits. The language of diplomacy reflected this power and superiority through expressions of deference and verbal flourishes that conveyed importance and dignity.

Diplomatic gifts were also seen as a means of affirming international relations and reflected a sense of appreciation and power. With the development of diplomatic protocols, the importance of official diplomatic visits and ceremonies representing political power and grandeur increased. These diplomatic practices reflect the transformation of diplomacy into an arena for displaying power and asserting control and sovereignty.[15]

However, diplomatic protocols had caused increased tensions between states and empires, as strict protocol practices and customs had led to diplomatic conflicts and escalating political tensions.[16] Thus, diplomatic practices in the mighty empires reflected power and political influence, but they also led to international problems and tensions that caused relations between states to deteriorate.

Revolutions and their impact on the diplomatic corps

The 19th century saw a series of political and social revolutions that had a profound impact on the international scene and the diplomatic corps. These revolutions posed a real challenge to existing political systems and great powers, leading to radical changes in diplomacy. [17] The effects of these revolutions varied from region to region.

In Europe, revolutions broke out that contributed to the weakening of the influence of the Ottoman and Austro-Hungarian empires and the displacement of many traditional capitals.[18] Meanwhile, in Latin America, numerous revolutions broke out against European colonialism, leading to the establishment of new states and structural changes in regional powers. 19] With all these revolutions affecting the diplomatic corps, international negotiations became more complex and difficult, and relations between states became more tense.[20]

The revolutions presented diplomats with new challenges and increased political pressure to find peaceful and sustainable solutions to conflicts. It is worth noting that the impact of the revolutions was not limited to the diplomatic arena but also extended to international law and human rights, prompting diplomats to rethink their strategies and practices.[21] Therefore, understanding the effects of revolutions on the diplomatic corps is essential to understanding the dynamics of diplomacy in the modern era.

Diplomacy in the 19th century: the expansion of geopolitics

During the 19th century, the world witnessed major political transformations that affected the diplomatic landscape. The 19th century saw a tremendous expansion in geopolitics and the emergence of new powers on the international stage. New empires began to establish themselves and expand their influence, leading to radical changes in the system of international relations.

Diplomacy played a crucial role in this context [22], as foreign relations experienced tremendous momentum and increasing tensions. International competition and regional conflicts escalated, leading to a redrawing of the political map of the world. As geopolitical differences and conflicts grew, it became harder for countries to understand each other, and international relations became more complicated. By analysing the diplomatic events of this period, we find that the expansion of geopolitics had a significant impact on the practices and contexts of international diplomacy.

The challenges and responsibilities facing diplomats increased, with the issues facing states becoming more complex and requiring decisive diplomatic solutions. Therefore, understanding the history of diplomacy during this period is vital to understanding modern and future diplomatic challenges.

References

History of Diplomacy

[1] Modern diplomacy owes important features to both the ancient Middle East and the classical periods of ancient Greece and the Roman Republic, challenging the notion of diplomacy as a single feature. This chapter discusses the evolution of diplomacy throughout history, noting that modern diplomacy derives important features from the ancient Middle East and the periods of ancient Greece, the Roman Republic, and the Roman Empire. Balzacq, Charillon, and Ramel address the concept of diplomacy, modifying definitions that rely on a single characteristic such as representation, communication, or negotiation. See:

Thierry Balzacq, Frédéric Charillon, and Frédéric Ramel. 'Introduction: History and Theories of Diplomacy.' *Global Diploma-*

cy (2019). https://doi.org/10.1007/978-3-030-28786-3_1.

[2] Paul Collins. 'From Egypt to Babylon: The International Age, 1550-500 BC.' (2007). https://doi.org/10.5860/choice.47-1013.

[3] R. Westbrook and Amarna. 'Babylonian Diplomacy in the Amarna Letters.' *Journal of the American Oriental Society*, 120 (2000): 377-382. https://doi.org/10.2307/606009.

[4] Marian H. Feldman. 'Assur Tomb 45 and the Birth of the Assyrian Empire.' *Bulletin of the American Schools of Oriental Research*, 343 (2006): 21 - 43. https://doi.org/10.1086/BASOR25066963.

[5] Khan, Uzma, Huili Wang, Zhongliang Cui, Abida Begum, Abdullah Mohamed, and Heesup Han. 2022. 'The Philosophical Thought of Confucius and Mencius, and the Concept of the Community of a Shared Future for Mankind' *Sustainability* 14, no. 16: 9854. https://doi.org/10.3390/su14169854

[6] K. Raaflaub. 'War and Peace in the Ancient World.' (2006). https://doi.org/10.1002/9780470774083.

[7] W. Roberts. 'The Evolution of Diplomacy.' *Mediterranean Quarterly*, 17 (2006): 55 - 64. https://doi.org/10.1215/10474552-2006-015.

This researcher explains that the word 'diplomacy' has Greek roots and was later used by the French to refer to the work of a negotiator acting on behalf of a sovereign. The research traces the history of diplomatic activity over at least two thousand years, noting the establishment of the first foreign ministry in Paris in 1626.

[8] Raymond Cohen. 'The great tradition: The spread of diplomacy in the ancient world.' *Diplomacy & Statecraft*, 12 (2001): 23 - 38. https://doi.org/10.1080/09592290108406186.

This research shows that diplomacy as we understand it today emerged in the third millennium BC in the ancient Near East, with the development of writing and urban culture. These traditions were transferred to the classical civilisations of Greece and Rome and continued to flourish in Byzantium, Rome and Venice, with the Renaissance providing the conditions for their spread.

[9] F. Adcock. 'The Development of Ancient Greek Diplomacy.' *Antiquity*, 17 (1948): 1-12. https://doi.org/10.3406/ANTIQ.1948.2822.

[10] Dover, Paul, and Hamish Scott. 'The Emergence of Diplomacy.' In The Oxford Handbook of Early Modern History 1350–1750. Vol. 2. Edited by Hamish Scott, 663–695. Oxford: Oxford University Press, 2015.

[11] Ibid.

[12] Dover, Paul, and Hamish Scott. (2015), op. cit.

[13] M. Akasha. 'Evolution of Diplomacy.' (2012). https://doi.org/10.2139/SSRN.2220467.

This research states that diplomacy is the second oldest profession, with evidence of diplomatic practices in ancient Egyptian, Greek, and Roman times. It points out that the origins of modern diplomacy can be traced back to the states of northern Italy and the early Renaissance. Diplomacy has evolved from ancient practices to modern forms, adapting to different political and economic contexts.

[14] Xiong, Qunrong. "International Exchanges and Cultural Communication in Chinese History." Lecture Notes on History, 2023.

[15] van Hoef, Y. Friendship among nations: History of a concept. *Contemp Polit Theory* **19** (Suppl 4), 231–234 (2020). https://doi.org/10.1057/s41296-019-00323-1

[16] Zhiyu, Xiong. "The Position and Function of Balance Diplomacy in the History of Modern International Relations." (2019).

[17] Bury, J.P.T. Diplomacy and Revolution: G.P. Gooch and the Genesis of History. London: Longman, 1974.

[18] Schulz, Matthias. Diplomacy and Revolutions: German Ambassadors and the Transformations of the International System, 1789-1919. Cambridge: Cambridge University Press, 2019.

[19] Pike, Fredrick B., ed. Diplomacy and Revolution in Latin America. Notre Dame, IN: University of Notre Dame Press, 1985.

[20] Katz, Friedrich. 'Diplomacy and Revolution: The Case of Mexico, 1910-1920.' Diplomatic History 13, no. 1 (1989): 19-37.

[21] J. Siracusa. '1. Evolution of diplomacy.' *Diplomatic History: A Very Short Introduction* (2010). https://doi.org/10.1093/ACTRADE/9780199588503.003.0001.

This researcher reviews the development of modern

diplomacy with a focus on diplomats and the art of treaty-making. He refers to peace treaties and international cooperation that have shaped the diplomatic landscape throughout history, such as the Treaties of Vienna (1815), Brest-Litovsk (1918) and Versailles (1919). The development of diplomacy, with its emphasis on treaty-making, has shaped the diplomatic landscape of human history, from the Congress of Vienna (1815) to the United Nations Charter (1948).

[22] Andrew Krischer and Hillard von Thiessen. 'Diplomacy in a Global Early Modernity: The Ambiguity of Sovereignty.' *The International History Review*, 41 (2018): 1100–1107. https://doi.org/10.1080/07075332.2018.1536674.

This research discusses the historical changes in European foreign relations in the early modern era and how global power relations have influenced modern diplomacy and foreign relations.

3
Human Rights Origins and Development
In International Community

Definition and importance of human rights

Human rights are fundamental to human societies, representing the basic rights to which every human being is entitled without discrimination or violation. The definition of human rights revolves around the idea of providing protection and respect to every individual as a human being, regardless of their cultural, religious or economic background.

The legal importance of human rights stems from their role in achieving justice and equality among individuals in society. Laws and systems based on human rights principles must ensure the safety of all individuals and protect their fundamental freedoms. From an ethical standpoint, the importance of human rights stems from the recognition of human value and respect for human dignity and freedom.

Human rights protect individuals from torture and injustice and promote dignified living and self-development. Hence, we find that failure to respect human rights leads to injustice, oppression and moral decay in society. Therefore, we must understand the definition and importance of human rights as a rule that refers to justice and morality, which must be at the core of human societies.

The historical roots of human rights in ancient societies

The roots of human rights go back to many ancient societies and civilisations, where ideas and principles very similar to what we know today as human rights were emerging.[1] In ancient times, there were concepts and values that promoted the individual's capacity for freedom, dignity and justice. For example, some ancient texts, such as the Code of Hammurabi, reflect concepts of social justice and are based on the idea of protecting the poor and oppressed.

In Greek civilisation, Greek philosophy focused on the concept of humanity and dignity, with philosophers such as Plato and Aristotle addressing issues related to human freedom and privacy. Through Roman thought, the concepts of citizenship and rights evolved to include broader segments of society.

Islamic civilisation also played a major role in the development of the concept of human rights, with Islamic law stipulating the rights, freedom, dignity and uniqueness of the individual. Islamic law considered human rights to be a fundamental issue and established rules and regulations to provide protection and justice for the individual. These historical examples indicate that the concept of human rights has deep historical roots in various ancient civilisations, highlighting the importance of this issue and its place in modern discussions and thinking about rights and freedoms.

The influence of European philosophies on the concept of human rights

Since the Renaissance and the Reformation, European philosophies have contributed significantly to the formulation of the modern concept of human rights.[2] Those times and the period that followed witnessed a revolution in moral and philosophical thinking, as philosophers and thinkers began to highlight the importance and dignity of the individual. Humanist thought was influenced by the works of philosophers such as Goethe, Kant, Rousseau, Voltaire and others, who fought to provide adequate protection for human rights as an integral part of human existence.

The French Revolution and the French Declaration of the Rights of Man and of the Citizen significantly advanced the official recognition of human rights.[3] In addition, European legal philosophies [4], such as natural rights and rational rights, discussed the philosophical foundations of human rights. [5] These philosophies contributed to the construction of the modern concept of human rights based on the values of justice, humanity, and human dignity.[6] Hence the importance of European philosophy and its profound influence on our understanding of human rights and their role in the international community.

The writing of the Universal Declaration of Human Rights and the work of the United Nations

The United Nations, influenced by European philosophies on the concept of human rights, played a decisive role in drafting the Universal Declaration of Human Rights, which marked a turning point in the history of human rights. There was a need for a declaration that would define the fundamental rights that should be guaranteed to every individual unconditionally and lay down international legal foundations for their protection and promotion. After the bloody conflicts that the world witnessed in the 20th century, it was urgent to draft a declaration that would protect all of humanity from the dangers of brutal abuses and violations of rights.

Efforts in this direction began after the Second World War, when the United Nations convened the San Francisco Conference in 1945 to draft the United Nations Charter and establish the international organisation with the aim of maintaining world peace and security. A committee was tasked with forming a human rights commission to draft a Universal Declaration of Human Rights.[7]

The Universal Declaration of Human Rights was adopted on 10 December 1948 by the United Nations General Assembly. [8] This declaration, which is considered a major historical achievement, recognises the human rights and fundamental freedoms that should be guaranteed to every individual unconditionally, whether in the political, social, economic or cultural sphere. The Universal Declaration of Human Rights contains 30 articles addressing individual rights and fundamental freedoms such as the right to life, liberty, equality, non-discrimination, education, and economic, social and cultural rights. These articles reflect universal human values and emphasise the values of justice and equality that should prevail in human societies.

The United Nations has played a prominent role in promoting action under the Declaration, setting out the objectives of promoting and protecting human rights through the establishment of international legal structures and cooperation with states in taking the necessary measures to implement these rights. The Office of the United Nations High Commissioner for Human Rights was also established to monitor developments in the field of human rights and work to promote them. In cooperation with other states and international organisations, the United Nations continues to strive to promote human culture and human rights at the international and local levels.

International agreements and protocols promoting human rights

Agreements and protocols drafted by the international community to promote the protection of these rights have transformed human rights into binding international law. International agreements and protocols are an essential part of the contemporary international legal system, which aims to ensure that human rights are respected and enforced throughout the world. [9] These agreements and protocols represent the commitment of member states to protect human rights and ensure a dignified life for individuals. [10] These agreements cover many human rights issues, such as women's rights, children's rights, refugee rights, and many others. These agreements aim to achieve sustainable progress in the protection of fundamental human rights, thereby promoting justice, equality, and economic prosperity.

The implementation of these agreements requires international cooperation and joint efforts to achieve their objectives and guarantee human rights for all individuals regardless of gender, race, religion, or social status. International human rights conventions and protocols are effective instruments for constructing a more inclusive and equitable world, wherein all individuals can exercise their fundamental rights free from discrimination or infringement.[11] Therefore, strengthening commitment to the implementation of these conventions and protocols remains an important challenge that requires continuous efforts by the international community and member states to move towards a world that respects and protects the human rights of all.

The rebirth of human rights in contemporary international law

Human rights are one of the most prominent topics in contemporary international law, having undergone remarkable developments in recent decades. With growing awareness of the importance of protecting human rights at the international level, new principles and laws have been adopted with the aim of promoting and protecting these fundamental rights. From a legal perspective, many countries and international organisations have witnessed new declarations and agreements relating to human rights, with new principles enshrined that aim to guarantee equality for all before the law and protect their fundamental rights without discrimination.

Perhaps the most prominent of these agreements is the Universal Declaration of Human Rights, issued by the United Nations in 1948, which is considered a fundamental reference in human rights issues worldwide. [12] In addition, international courts have seen a significant development in their role in protecting human rights, with the formation of special courts and international tribunals to hear cases of human rights violations at the global level. [13]

These courts work to enforce international laws and global humanitarian standards, and are responsible for holding violators accountable and ensuring justice and compensation for victims. It is undeniable that the rebirth of human rights in contemporary international law reflects the social and political transformations in the world [14]. It reflects the ongoing struggle to guarantee human rights and dignity at the global level. Despite the challenges and difficulties, [15] this new birth represents a promising start towards an equal and just world that fulfils humanity's aspirations for justice, freedom and dignity.

International courts and their role in protecting human rights

International courts play a vital role in protecting human rights at the international level, as their efforts represent a turning point in the application of human rights laws. In light of the cultural and political challenges in different societies around the world, international courts seek to achieve justice and ensure respect for the human rights of all individuals, regardless of their nationality or cultural background.[16]

The International Court of Justice and other international courts are prominent examples in this regard, as they resolve international disputes related to human rights and adopt positions that emphasise the importance of respecting these rights and applying relevant international laws. [17] These courts also seek to raise global awareness of the importance of protecting human rights and provide legal support to victims and affected communities.

Through in-depth analysis of human rights issues and international law, international courts contribute to building a strong legal foundation for the protection of human rights and to establishing international standards that guide the behaviour of states and individuals towards more effective commitments. [18] These judicial efforts by international courts are a vital foundation for promoting a culture of respect and promotion of human rights in our societies today.

Cultural and political challenges in the global application of human rights

Cultural and political challenges are among the most significant factors affecting the application of human rights at the international and local levels. In the context of globalisation and cultural diversity, the concept of human rights often conflicts with various values and beliefs that may contradict certain aspects of it.[19]

International communities need to address these challenges seriously and constructively to ensure comprehensive protection of human rights. Various political factors complement cultural challenges, as there may be political and economic interests that conflict with the implementation and respect of human rights. Decisive steps must be taken to overcome these obstacles and strengthen the commitment to implementing human rights without bias or discrimination.

International organisations and national governments must work together to raise awareness of the importance of human rights and promote a culture of rights at the international level, adopting policies and programmes that encourage respect for and implementation of those rights without exception. This is a real challenge that requires joint and sustained efforts from all actors in the international community.

Human rights in times of crisis: from wars to pandemics

Humanity is most clearly evident in times of crisis. When wars and pandemics strike humanity, the issue of human rights emerges more strongly than ever. Ordinary citizens who find themselves in armed conflicts experience severe suffering that exceeds their capacity to endure. Their fundamental rights to life, safety and freedom are in constant danger, and they are exposed to the risks of displacement, hunger and constant violations of their human dignity. In these difficult times, international communities have a responsibility to find just and equitable solutions that restore human dignity and promote forgotten rights. However, these challenges do not end with the end of armed conflicts [20] but continue following epidemics and natural disasters.

Health threats pose new challenges to human rights [21], as life, health, and freedom are put at risk, and the poor and marginalised bear the brunt of crises. In this context, diplomats and international decision-makers must work together to develop policies and procedures that ensure the protection of human rights in the face of various crises, provide the necessary support to those affected, and promote social and economic sustainability. This is an opportunity for the international community to show solidarity and humanity in the face of adversity and to work hard towards realising human rights aspirations, thereby achieving security and dignity for every individual in this volatile world.

Conclusion: The future of human rights in a changing world

Human rights have been greatly affected in recent decades by rapid and growing developments in the world. Following social, economic and technological transformations, the international community faces new challenges in ensuring the continued protection and respect of human rights at the national and international levels. Since the adoption of the Universal Declaration of Human Rights in 1948, the world has witnessed tremendous developments in the field of human rights and international action to promote and protect human rights.

However, current challenges and crises require new visions and strategies to guarantee human rights in our time. In the future, we must seriously consider how to address emerging challenges that may affect human rights, including climate change, new technologies and global health crises. We must also develop robust plans to promote human rights in political, economic, and social processes. It is also essential that we move towards building greater international solidarity that promotes human rights and provides support to developing countries and those affected by humanitarian crises. International efforts must be directed towards providing assistance and coordination to address global challenges in a manner that preserves human dignity and ensures access to justice and equality for all. In this context, states' diplomacy and foreign policy must be based on human rights principles and their commitment to promoting international cooperation to protect human rights everywhere.

The international community must work together to combat all forms of persecution and discrimination and to guarantee the rights of vulnerable and marginalised groups. It is important to support research and innovation in the field of human rights and to raise awareness of the importance of human rights in achieving sustainable development. Public and economic policies must support ethical principles and human values and seek to provide equal opportunities for all without discrimination. Ultimately, we must always remember that the protection of human rights is the responsibility of all individuals and societies alike, and it is a shared responsibility that we must all bear. Human rights are the foundation of dignity, justice and peace in a changing world, and we must work together for a future that respects the rights of all.

References

Human Rights Origins and Development

[1] See Chapter 1 of this study.

[2] Buergenthal, T. "The Normative and Institutional Evolution of International Human Rights." Human Rights Quarterly 19 (1997): 703–23.

This article analyses the different stages in the development of contemporary international human rights law, beginning with the United Nations Charter, which laid the foundation for modern international human rights law.

[3] Kundal, Navjeet Sidhu. "The Evolution and Impact of Human Rights: From Ancient Origins to Modern Challenges." International Journal of Science and Research (IJSR), 2023.

This article traces the historical trajectory of human rights, from their ancient origins to their modern manifestations. It explores the philosophical foundations and evolution of human rights instruments such as the Magna Carta and the American Declaration of Independence.

[4] Sossai, M. "Catholicism and the Evolution of International Law Studies in Italy," 215–33, 2020.

This study examines the influence of Catholicism on the development of international law studies in Italy, including its impact on the concept of human rights.

[5] David S. Weissbrodt, F. N. Aoláin and Mary Rumsey. 'The development of international human rights law.' (2017). https://doi.org/10.4324/9781315086750.

[6] Drozenová, Wendy. "Ethical Foundations of Jacques Maritain's and Michael Novak's Conception of Human Rights." Ethics & Bioethics 13 (2023): 127–37. This article analyses the ethical foundations of the concept of human rights in the work of European philosophers Jacques Maritain and Michael Novak.

[7] Beall, Katherine M. "The Global South and Global Human Rights: International Responsibility for the Right to Development." Third World Quarterly 43 (2022): 2337–56.

[7] Beall, Katherine M. "The Global South and Global Human Rights: International Responsibility for the Right to Development." Third World Quarterly 43 (2022): 2337–56.

This article explores the role of the Global South in shaping the concept of universal human rights, including their contribution to the drafting of the Universal Declaration of Human Rights.

[8] Johannes Morsink. 'The Universal Declaration of Human Rights: Origins, Drafting, and Intent.' American Journal of Legal History, 43 (1999): 346–347. https://doi.org/10.9783/9780812200416.

The Universal Declaration of Human Rights, adopted in 1948, forms the moral backbone of more than two hundred human rights instruments.

[9] M. Lesch and Nina Reiners. 'Informal human rights law-making: How treaty bodies use 'General Comments' to develop international law.' *Global Constitutionalism* (2023). https://doi.org/10.1017/s2045381723000023.

Treaty bodies use 'General Comments' to informally shape international human rights law, relying on their networks and expertise to counter opposition from powerful states.

[10] Schabas, W. "The Customary International Law of Human Rights," 2021.

This book discusses the development of customary international human rights law, including major international conventions and protocols.

[11] E. Neumayer. 'Do International Human Rights Treaties Improve Respect for Human Rights?' Journal of Conflict Resolution, 49 (2005): 925–953. https://doi.org/10.1177/0022002705281667.

International human rights treaties can improve respect for human rights in more democratic countries or those with strong civil societies, but may have no effect in authoritarian regimes with weak civil societies.

[12] Gleider Hernández. '16. International human rights and refugee law.' *International Law* (2019).

https://doi.org/10.1093/HE/9780198748830.003.0016.
The Universal Declaration of Human Rights and other international human rights treaties have contributed to the formation of international law, while regional frameworks such as the European, American and African human rights conventions have also contributed to providing protection.

[13] Kuzenko, U. "Universal Declaration of Human Rights as a Source of Universal International Legal Standards of Human Rights," 36–42, 2020.

This study analyses the Universal Declaration of Human Rights as an international legal instrument that laid the foundations for the modern democratic status of human beings and their fundamental rights and freedoms.

[14] Schulze, S. "Hansa Mehta and the Universal Declaration of Human Rights," 66:254–58, 2018. This study focuses on Hansa Mehta's role in drafting the Universal Declaration of Human Rights, highlighting the contribution of the Global South to this process.

[15] Sarkin, J., and Ross Callum Capazorio. "The Syrian Conflict as a Test Case for the Limits of the International Community and International Law: Global Politics and State Sovereignty Versus Human Rights Protection." *Human Rights Quarterly* 44 (2022): 476–513.

This article uses the Syrian conflict as a case study to explore the limits of the international community and international law in protecting human rights in the modern era.

[16] Moreira, F. "The Advisory Role of International Courts in the Evolution of Human Rights Law." Juridical Tribune, 2023.

This study examines the advisory role of international courts in the evolution of contemporary human rights law.

[17] Loger, J. "Practice, Evolution and Protection of Human Rights through the International Court of Justice Jurisprudence." American Yearbook of International Law, 2023.

This article analyses the role of the International Court of Justice in the development and protection of human rights through its jurisprudence.

[18] Murray, Daragh. "Organising Rebellion: Non-State Armed Groups under International Humanitarian Law, Human Rights Law, and International Criminal Law Tilman Rodenhauser *." Revue Internationale de La Croix-Rouge 101 (2019): 377–82.

This review discusses the role of international courts in applying international humanitarian law and human rights law to non-state armed groups.

[19] Almahfali, Mohammed, M. Levine, and Abdulghani Muthanna. "Mapping Arabic Human Rights Discourse: A Thematic Review." International Journal of Human Rights 28 (2023): 197–219.

This review provides a comprehensive overview of human rights discourse in the Arab world, highlighting the cultural and political challenges in applying human rights.

[20] Voloshchuk, Oksana, Viktoriia Kolesnyk, A. Shevchuk, O. Yushchyk, and P. Krainii. "Human Rights Protection in the Context of Combating Terrorism: Problems of Finding the Optimal Balance." Revista Amazonía Investiga, 2021.

This article examines the challenges of protecting human rights in the context of combating terrorism, highlighting the tensions between security and human rights in times of crisis.

[21] Wewerinke-Singh, M. "Pandemics, Planetary Health and Human Rights." Max Planck Yearbook of United Nations Law Online, 2021.

This study explores the relationship between pandemics, planetary health, and human rights, with a focus on the role of global solidarity and international cooperation.

4
The Relationship Between Diplomacy and Human Rights
Interactions and Challenges

Defining the Relationship Between Diplomacy and Human Rights

The relationship between diplomacy and human rights is a complex issue that raises many questions about how diplomatic relations can strengthen or weaken human rights. From the dawn of ancient civilisations to the modern era, diplomatic relations and their interaction with human rights have undergone significant developments and radical transformations.

Diplomacy has always been accompanied by human rights issues and related conflicts, and it has been a mechanism for influencing human rights, both positively and negatively. Diplomacy is one of the main tools for interaction between states and societies at the regional and international levels, and it has had a significant impact on shaping modern concepts of human rights.

Historically, diplomatic interactions have taken many forms, ranging from political negotiations and conflict mediation to economic sanctions and regional and international alliances, all of which have been influenced by the extent to which human rights are respected in the countries concerned. Research on this topic requires a comprehensive understanding of the effects of diplomacy on human rights, as well as a careful analysis of the factors that sometimes lead to the erosion of human rights as a result of political or economic interests. Identifying the true relationship between diplomacy and human rights is vital to understanding how diplomatic factors affect fundamental human rights and how to strike a balance between them.

The historical context of the interaction between diplomacy and human rights

The relationship between diplomacy and human rights is one of the most complex areas of the international arena, based on a long history of interaction and conflict. We have noted that the history of this relationship dates back to ancient times, when ancient nations and civilisations had their own systems for expressing international relations and dealing with human rights issues. Since then, diplomacy and human rights have undergone significant transformations, influenced by major historical events. The interaction between diplomacy and human rights has evolved considerably over the past 70 years, since the adoption of the Universal Declaration of Human Rights in 1948. [1] Some of the key historical developments include the following:

- The 1960s and 1970s saw an increasing focus on human rights in international diplomacy, particularly in relation to decolonisation efforts.

- In the 1970s, there was a proliferation of non-governmental organisations and transnational activist networks focused on human rights.

- The Helsinki Process in the 1970s made human rights a permanent part of the conversation between East and West.

- President Carter made human rights a central focus of US foreign policy in the late 1970s [5].

With the end of the Cold War in the early 1990s, the world witnessed major shifts in international relations, including an increased focus on human rights. This period was pivotal in reshaping international politics and directing attention to human rights issues.

Our research highlights the following key findings:

Increased focus on democracy and the global economy:

After the end of the Cold War, governments that became more democratic or increased their participation in the global economy showed higher levels of respect for human rights, particularly regarding not imprisoning citizens for political reasons. [6]

The impacts of non-governmental organisations and cross-border activism:

The end of the Cold War paved the way for non-governmental organisations to disseminate human rights ideas and practices globally, thereby contributing to the international advancement of human rights. [7]

Ongoing human rights challenges:

Despite improvements in some aspects of human rights, violations such as torture, enforced disappearances, and extrajudicial killings continued at roughly the same rates after the end of the Cold War. [8]

Inconsistencies in the enforcement of human rights:

The end of the Cold War led to increased international interest in human rights, but it also revealed contradictions in the application of these rights, as some countries continued to violate human rights despite their international commitments. [9]

Cultural and ideological impact:

Ideas about human rights became influential factors in international and domestic politics, particularly in Eastern Europe, where opposition groups began to expose human rights violations by their governments. [10]

In conclusion, the end of the Cold War was an important turning point in increasing the focus on human rights in international relations. Despite improvements in some areas, challenges and violations continued. However, non-governmental organisations and cross-border activism have played a significant role in spreading and promoting human rights, although inconsistencies in their implementation remain.

The most important international conventions and their role in shaping concepts

International conventions are one of the most important ways to define and shape ideas about human rights and how diplomacy can help promote them. These conventions represent an international legal reference for the protection and promotion of human rights and constitute a framework that guides diplomatic relations between states. Among these conventions is the Charter of the United Nations, which is considered one of the most important international treaties defining the human rights and fundamental freedoms that must be respected. [11] These conventions also seek to promote the concept of justice, equality [12], and freedom for all without discrimination based on race, religion, gender, or any other consideration. [13]

In addition, these international charters emphasise the need to respect human rights in all circumstances and situations and define the responsibilities that states must bear towards their people. Diplomats must take these charters into account when promoting human rights during international deliberations and negotiations. Understanding these conventions and their role in shaping concepts of human rights contributes to promoting diplomatic reforms and ensuring justice and equality. Since diplomacy plays a pivotal role in the impact of international policies on human rights, understanding and appreciating the role of these conventions serve to promote fundamental rights for all.

The Impact of International Policy on Human Rights

International policy provides an important framework that defines the interaction between states and international organisations on human rights issues. The impact of international policy on human rights can be a mixture of challenges and opportunities. Political decisions made by governments can have a significant impact on the rights of individuals within countries and at the international level. [14] Some international policies focus on promoting and protecting human rights through international agreements and conventions, such as the Universal Declaration of Human Rights and United Nations conventions.

On the other hand, some policies are contrary to human rights and lead to widespread violations, such as repression, discrimination and internal wars. [15] Determining the extent to which international policies affect human rights requires a comprehensive understanding of international dynamics and conflicting interests between states. Political, economic, and cultural factors play a decisive role in determining state policies and their impact on human rights.[16] In this context, diplomacy plays a crucial role in dealing with the impact of international policies on human rights.

Diplomats work to shape international policies in a way that serves human rights and achieves social justice through negotiation and influence in international forums and institutions. [17] We cannot overlook the challenges that international policies pose to human rights. The interests of states often conflict with the protection of human rights, and this is where the conflict between national objectives in their various forms becomes apparent. [18] Addressing these challenges requires influencing the formulation of international policies in a way that preserves the morality and humanity of international relations and contributes to the promotion of human rights.

The role of diplomacy in addressing human rights crises

The role of diplomacy in addressing human rights crises is one of the most important roles that diplomacy plays in the international arena, as human rights crises are among the most serious situations that any country can face. [19] Diplomacy is an essential means of dealing with crises due to its ability to use methods such as negotiation, mediation and international pressure to resolve them peacefully and effectively.

Providing protection to civilians and working to stop human rights violations is an essential part of the role of diplomacy in addressing human rights crises. [20]

We can make significant progress in protecting victims and influencing the parties to the conflict by adopting innovative diplomatic strategies. In addition, diplomacy works with international organisations and humanitarian institutions to provide necessary support and assistance to victims and those affected by human rights crises.

Diplomacy also maintains constant communication with governments and relevant parties to contribute to the development of effective policies and programmes to address these crises and prevent their escalation in the future. Thus, the role of diplomacy in addressing human rights crises demonstrates the great importance of diplomats in achieving reconciliation and peace and promoting human rights in affected communities. Overall, this role is particularly evident when two methods are used:

- A tool for pressure: Diplomacy can be an effective tool for pressuring intransigent regimes to respect human rights through the use of diplomatic tools to promote these rights. [21]
- Promoting human rights: Using diplomatic tools to promote human rights abroad, where human rights issues can be part of other foreign policy objectives. [22]

Key obstacles to advancing human rights via diplomacy

Promoting human rights through diplomacy is essential but complex and faces many challenges and difficulties. Diplomacy aimed at protecting and promoting human rights faces multiple challenges, including political and cultural constraints, pressure from national and international interests, and resistance from some repressive regimes and authoritarian governments. [23] These key challenges are a major obstacle to efforts to promote human rights through diplomacy.

Note that promoting human rights necessitates effective international partnerships and strong cooperation between states and international human rights organisations. Hence, the flourishing of the international system and economic integration between states can contribute to alleviating some of these challenges and strengthening the role of diplomacy in promoting human rights. Nevertheless, there remains an urgent need to resume efforts to strike a balance between national and international interests and human rights and to seek to overcome the obstacles facing diplomacy in this field.

Diplomats and foreign policy leaders should adopt balanced and prudent strategies that transcend the political and cultural difficulties that hinder the promotion of human rights through diplomatic channels. In addition, it is essential that the international community provide the necessary support to human rights organisations and strengthen their role in achieving tangible progress in promoting human rights through diplomatic channels.

Greater efforts must be made to enhance transparency and accountability in international relations and international cooperation to address the challenges and obstacles that hinder the role of diplomacy in promoting human rights. [24] States and the international community must work in a spirit of cooperation and embrace universal human values to address key challenges and strengthen the role of diplomacy as an effective means of promoting human rights around the world.

Examples of interactions between diplomats and human rights organisations

Interaction between diplomats and human rights organisations is a fundamental aspect of the pursuit of justice and the protection of human rights at the national and international levels. For decades, independent human rights organisations and international organisations have worked to monitor human rights violations and raise awareness about the importance of respecting these fundamental rights. [25] In this context, diplomacy has engaged closely with these organisations to support human rights protections and promote social justice.

The importance of interactions between diplomats and human rights organisations is evident in the effective impact they can have on international policies and national legislation in the field of human rights. [26] Diplomats can convey these concerns and challenges to the highest official levels within governments and international institutions, thereby promoting measures and policies that protect human rights and work towards achieving social justice. On the other hand, human rights organisations provide the necessary support and information [27] to enable diplomats to better understand issues and potential human rights violations, thereby allowing them to direct their efforts and initiatives more effectively.

These organisations also provide necessary support in the area of documentation and evidence, which contributes to supporting diplomatic campaigns. A concrete example of effective interaction between diplomats and human rights organisations is the intervention of many embassies and diplomatic missions in defending persecuted human rights defenders, supporting them and protecting them from harassment and unlawful arrests. In addition, many international meetings and conferences witness cooperation based on trust and understanding among diplomats and human rights organisations to discuss ways to improve the human rights situation in various countries. In conclusion, interactions between diplomats and human rights organisations appear to be integral parts of the process of supporting human rights and promoting justice. This cooperation is one of the pillars of building sustainable international relations based on respect for the fundamental rights of all human beings.

The role of international cooperation in supporting human rights

International cooperation plays a vital role in supporting human rights around the world. Coordinating efforts between states and international organisations enhances the impact and effectiveness of human rights protection. [28] This cooperation aims to promote international human rights standards and ensure that they are respected throughout the world. This includes joint action in areas such as fundamental freedoms, the protection of vulnerable groups, and combating persecution and discrimination. [29]

International cooperation raises awareness of the importance of human rights and their role in building strong and prosperous societies. It also works to create international laws and systems that protect and enforce human rights. International cooperation requires consensus among states and the exchange of knowledge and expertise to achieve common goals in the field of human rights. By coordinating efforts and providing mutual support, international cooperation can achieve positive and sustainable results in the protection of human rights globally.

Legal frameworks and their impact on diplomatic policy

Legal frameworks are among the most important factors influencing diplomatic policies related to human rights. These frameworks form the basis for interactions and joint efforts among states and international organisations to promote and protect human rights through diplomatic channels. The adoption and respect of these legal frameworks reflect states' commitment to achieving fundamental human rights principles in the context of international relations.

One of the main aspects is the impact of legal frameworks on the formulation of diplomatic relations between states, as these legal frameworks define possible avenues for international cooperation in the field of human rights and identify possible mechanisms for negotiation and cooperation. For instance, these legal frameworks outline the human rights obligations of states that are part of the European Union.[30]

Furthermore, legal frameworks serve as a framework for accountability, as states commit to implementing and respecting human rights laws and to reporting regularly on those commitments. Commitment to legal frameworks can be a motivation for developing effective diplomatic strategies to support human rights at the international level, except for economic issues and the interpretation of social justice in liberal states. These often constitute a contradiction that renders commitments meaningless. [31]

Recommendations for strengthening the relationship between diplomacy and human rights in the future

We can use experience as a valuable asset to formulate future recommendations for enhancing the relationship between diplomacy and human rights. The role that states play on the international stage has a significant impact on the development and promotion of the concept of human rights. Therefore, strengthening international cooperation and increasing coordination between states to protect human rights is vital.

There should be serious investment in improving diplomatic capacities related to human rights, whether through the development of specialised training programmes or the formation of diplomatic cadres specialised in human rights issues. Consideration should also be given to strengthening coordination between diplomats and human rights institutions and organisations to ensure the exchange of information and expertise and joint action to achieve common goals. In this context, it is also important to encourage the role of civil society in promoting human rights and contributing to the formulation of related diplomatic policies.

Furthermore, technology can be a powerful ally in promoting human rights if it can be used to monitor violations, document cases, and raise awareness about them. Diplomacy should embrace technology in a positive and effective manner to achieve human rights goals. Ultimately, we must bear in mind that human rights are a humanitarian issue before they are a diplomatic one, and that diplomats and decision-makers must work earnestly to promote these fundamental values and principles.

References

The Relationship Between Diplomacy and Human Rights

[1] Yücel, Zeynep. "FROM NATURAL LAW TO UNIVERSAL DECLARATIONS: IMPLICATIONS FOR INTERNATIONAL HUMAN RIGHTS TREATIES AND THE RESPONSIBILITY TO PROTECT". Journal of Management and Economics Research 21, no. 4 (January 2024): 54-87. https://doi.org/10.11611/yead.1307685

[2] Rinaldi, Alberto. "The Making of International Human Rights: The 1960s, Decolonisation, and the Reconstruction of Global Values." Nordic Journal of Human Rights 40 (2022): 588–90.

[3] Grealy, David, and J. Gaskarth. "Human Rights and British Foreign Policy: Case Studies in Middle Power Diplomacy." Cambridge Review of International Affairs 36 (2023): 467–73.

[4] Ibid.

[5] Keys, B. "'Something to Boast About': Western Enthusiasm for Carter's Human Rights Diplomacy," 2016.

[6] David Cingranelli and David L. Richards. 'Respect for Human Rights after the End of the Cold War.' *Journal of Peace Research*, 36 (1999): 511 - 534. https://doi.org/10.1177/0022343399036005002.

[7] Mark Goodale. 'Toward a Critical Anthropology of Human Rights.' *Current Anthropology*, 47 (2006): 485 - 511. https://doi.org/10.1086/503061.

[8] R. Foot. 'The Cold War and human rights.' (2010): 445–465. https://doi.org/10.1017/CHOL9780521837217.022.

[9] R. Brier. 'Broadening the Cultural History of the Cold War: The Emergence of the Polish Workers' Defence Committee and the Rise of Human Rights.' *Journal of Cold War Studies*, 15 (2013): 104–127. https://doi.org/10.1162/JCWS_a_00396.

[10] Ibid.

[11] Yücel, Zeynep. "A Historical Framework for the Concept of Human Rights." Yönetim ve Ekonomi Araştırmaları Dergisi, 2023.

[12] Papastamou, Andreas. "Economic Diplomacy and Human Rights: In Search of a Democratic Framework." Rocznik Administracji Publicznej, 2022.

[13] Makhija, Heena. "India and Human Rights Diplomacy at the United Nations: The Discourse on Torture." Jadavpur Journal of International Relations 26 (2022): 208–26.

[14] Fitria, Naeli. "Exploring the Impact of Human Rights on Diplomatic Relations: A Comparative Analysis of State Interactions." COMSERVA: Jurnal Penelitian Dan Pengabdian Masyarakat, 2023.

[15] Anupama Ghosal and Sreeja Pal. 'The Politics of Human Rights Diplomacy.' *Jadavpur Journal of International Relations*, 25 (2020): 101–123. https://doi.org/10.1177/0973598420943437.

[16] Regimes that violate human rights tend to cause international instability, making concern for human rights legitimate because of its impact on international relations. Foreign policy tools, non-governmental organisations, the business community, and the media all play a role in promoting human rights and addressing crises, with the United Nations playing a crucial role.

R. Mullerson. 'Human Rights Diplomacy.' (1997). https://doi.org/10.4324/9781315005188.

[17] International cooperation: Human rights issues can motivate countries to build international cooperation, as was the case in South Africa during apartheid, where human rights played a major role in improving diplomatic relations and transitioning to a democratic system. See:

Naeli Fitria. "Exploring the Impact of Human Rights on Diplomatic Relations: A Comparative Analysis of State Interactions. " *COMSERVA : Jurnal Penelitian dan Pengabdian Masyarakat* (2023). https://doi.org/10.59141/comserva.v3i1.755.

[18] Trade and national security issues often take

precedence over human rights issues in the formulation of foreign policy, leading to human rights violations being ignored in favour of respect for sovereignty and non-interference, even though diplomacy has the power to pressure rogue regimes to respect human rights. See:

Source cited. (Anupama Ghosal and Sreeja Pal. (2020

[19] Thuzar, M. "Myanmar and the Responsibility to Protect: Principles, Precedents, and Practicalities." Journal of International Peacekeeping, 2023.

[20] Rashid, Sid. "Preventive Diplomacy, Mediation and the Responsibility to Protect in Libya: A Missed Opportunity for Canada?" International Mediation in a Fragile World 19 (2013): 39–52.

[21] Anupama Ghosal and Sreeja Pal. (2020): Source cited above.

[22] R. Mullerson. 'Human Rights Diplomacy.' (1997). https://doi.org/10.4324/9781315005188.

[23] Bakke, Kristin M., Neil J. Mitchell, and Hannah M. Smidt. "When States Crack Down on Human Rights Defenders." International Studies Quarterly, 2019.

[24] Alston, Philip. "The Populist Challenge to Human Rights." Journal of Human Rights Practice 9 (2017): 1–15.

[25] Amores, Recalde, and C. Veronica. "Integrating a Gender Perspective and a Human Rights-Based Approach in Institutional Settings: An Assessment of Gender Equality Policies and Practices of the United Nations Office of the High Commissioner for Human Rights-OHCHR," 2013.

[26] Human rights diplomacy includes the role of ambassadors, small states, the European Union, and various United Nations bodies, as well as the role of non-governmental organisations and national human rights institutions. See:
Amrei Mueller, Michael O'flaherty, Zdzisław Kędzia and G. Ulrich. 'Human rights diplomacy: contemporary perspectives.' (2011). https://doi.org/10.1163/EJ.9789004195165.I-301

[27] Meier, B., Dabney P. Evans, M. Kavanagh, J. Keralis, and Gabriel Armas-Cardona. "Human Rights in Public Health." Health and Human Rights: An International Journal 20 (2018): 85–91.

[28] Amrei Mueller, Michael O'flaherty, Zdzisław Kędzia and G. Ulrich.(2011). Source cited.

[29] Amores, Recalde, and C. Veronica. 2013. Source cited.

[30] Bartels, L. "The EU's Human Rights Obligations in Relation to Policies with Extraterritorial Effects." European Journal of International Law 25 (2014): 1071–91.

[31] Nolan, A., and J. P. Bohoslavsky. "Human Rights and Economic Policy Reforms." International Journal of Human Rights 24 (2020): 1247–67.

5
Diplomacy as a Tool for Defending Human Rights

Introduction on the importance of diplomacy in defending human rights

Diplomacy is one of the most important means of negotiation and influence between different countries and societies and is of great importance in preserving and promoting human rights. It is the main tool for defending the values of justice, freedom and equality in the fields of international conflicts and negotiations. Diplomacy is based on a set of principles and foundations that enable it to contribute to achieving balance and understanding between conflicting parties and to move towards finding peaceful solutions.

This research explores fundamental concepts such as the concept of international relations and their objectives, the role of diplomatic negotiations in achieving stability and international peace, and cooperation between states to promote human rights. Highlighting the importance of using diplomatic tools reveals their vital role in achieving balance and justice in an international community that depends on interaction and cooperation between different states and peoples. This review shows that diplomacy is not merely a mechanism for resolving international conflicts, but also an effective means of defending human rights and promoting the values of justice and freedom.

Rooting concepts: the foundations and principles of diplomacy

Diplomacy is a fundamental basis of international relations. It is an art and a science that aims to regulate communication and interaction between states and societies. The secret of diplomacy's success lies in its ability to achieve common interests and goals without causing conflict or confrontation. Accordingly, these concepts are based on a set of fundamental values, such as honesty, clarity, and mutual respect among the parties involved in the diplomatic process.

Diplomacy must be based on human rights principles, which require respect for human dignity and the fundamental human rights of all individuals, regardless of any political or economic considerations. Based on this, diplomacy seeks to promote peace, security, and social justice through negotiations, understanding, and cooperation.

Diplomatic concepts and principles are effective tools for maintaining world peace, achieving international balance, and protecting fundamental rights and freedoms. Therefore, the lofty humanitarian goals of international relations and bilateral cooperation connect with the concept of diplomacy in the defence of human rights.

Bilateral cooperation and its impact on the promotion of fundamental rights

When we discuss bilateral cooperation between states in the context of human rights, we draw inspiration from a concept that is well established in modern diplomacy. [1] Bilateral cooperation is considered one of the most important means of promoting and protecting human rights in the international community. The essence of bilateral cooperation lies in the partnership between states to exchange expertise and experiences in the field of promoting fundamental rights for all. It reflects the spirit of solidarity and cooperation between states and reinforces joint efforts to improve humanitarian conditions worldwide.

This cooperation, which extends to various fields, has a positive and tangible impact on the promotion of fundamental rights.[2] By reviewing successful experiences, we can see how countries participating in this cooperation can pursue joint policies and programmes focused on promoting the civil, political, economic, social and cultural rights of all members of society. Effective bilateral action also demonstrates the importance of cooperation in developing internal laws and regulations that guarantee the protection and respect of human rights and freedoms. [3] It brings about tangible transformations in the human rights system at the national, regional and international levels.

On the other hand, bilateral cooperation also demonstrates the power of partnership in addressing the complex human rights challenges that states may face. [4] Through the exchange of experiences and cooperation in areas such as the pursuit of justice and legal system reform, countries engaged in such cooperation can effectively address common challenges and achieve significant progress in promoting human rights and combating injustice and oppression. So, bilateral cooperation is an important and useful way to protect human rights and work towards long-term peace and development.

The role of international treaties and agreements in supporting human rights

Since ancient times, international treaties have had an important influence on establishing relations between nations and defining the mutual rights and obligations of states. The application and guarantee of human rights principles requires strong and effective international agreements that ensure commitment to those principles at the global level. [5] The United Nations International Covenant on Economic, Social, and Cultural Rights and the International Covenant on Civil and Political Rights are among the most prominent international documents that promote human rights and lay the foundations for international cooperation in this field.

States' commitment to the provisions of these treaties represents an effective step towards promoting human rights and providing more effective protection for individuals, both within the borders of each individual state and in the context of international cooperation and interaction. [6] Furthermore, international treaties and conventions can contribute to promoting international dialogue and understanding on human rights issues and providing a clear legal framework for their protection.

Commitment to these treaties helps build bridges of trust between states and strike a balance between national sovereignty and international responsibility for human rights. Thus, international treaties and agreements play a vital and necessary role in supporting and promoting human rights at the national and international levels.

Diplomatic dialogue and its role in resolving human rights disputes

In the diplomatic arena, dialogue is an effective mechanism for resolving human rights disputes. Dialogue is fundamental to directing efforts towards finding sustainable and just solutions to complex disputes affecting societies and individuals. The mission of diplomacy is to promote the values of justice and fundamental rights, which means embracing dialogue as a vital tool in achieving these goals. Diplomatic dialogue serves two fundamental purposes: to strike a balance between the various conflicting parties and to achieve the goal of protecting human rights.

During dialogues, diplomats highlight the importance of open dialogue and cooperation in finding solutions that preserve the dignity and rights of individuals. They also strive to promote peace and stability, which are the foundations for achieving human rights. This phenomenon highlights the role of diplomatic dialogue in defusing conflicts and reaching settlements that meet the aspirations of communities and preserve their fundamental rights.

Furthermore, it demonstrates the role of dialogue in engaging the international community as a whole in supporting humanitarian causes and promoting the exchange of ideas and experiences to achieve positive change in the field of human rights. Over time, it has become necessary to maximise the use of diplomatic dialogue to achieve a positive balance in international relations and contribute to the attainment of justice and peace that promote human rights.

Notable diplomatic successes in the field of human rights

In some cases, diplomatic efforts have led to notable successes in the field of human rights. Observing the effective use of diplomacy in defending human rights and bringing about positive change is fascinating. [7] Several case studies can be cited to highlight specific successes around the world. These studies may include human rights cases that have been addressed through diplomatic intervention, as well as political and diplomatic efforts to achieve justice and protect the fundamental rights of individuals and communities. The issue of racial discrimination in South Africa, where international pressure led to the end of the abhorrent apartheid system, serves as one example. [8]

International efforts regarding the Palestinian issue and the role of diplomacy in influencing the humanitarian situation in the occupied territories can also be considered a vivid example, despite the obstacles that prevented the Israeli aggression on Gaza from being stopped at a time when the number of victims was increasing at an alarming rate. We can also review the role of diplomacy in promoting human rights during humanitarian interventions aimed at stopping violations and providing assistance. In addition, the research may address human rights cases in which diplomacy has been successful in resolving or has made tangible progress in improving human rights conditions. The State of Qatar has a long and distinguished record in this field.

In general, analysis of specific diplomatic successes demonstrates the importance of these efforts in defending human rights, achieving justice, and promoting humanitarian principles around the world.

Challenges and obstacles facing diplomats

In the field of diplomacy, diplomats face multiple challenges and obstacles in defending human rights. The diplomatic arena is a complex international environment permeated by political, economic, and social conflicts. Each country has its own history, culture, and priorities, which adds diversity and complexity to the task of diplomats in addressing human rights issues.

One of the main challenges diplomats face is pressure from foreign political and economic interests, as they discover themselves torn between their commitment to protecting human rights and maintaining vital international relations. [9] This contradiction puts them in a difficult position, where they must strike a balance between their commitment to values and principles and national and international interests.

Furthermore, diplomats face challenges in gathering and verifying information, especially when dealing with countries that lack transparency or engage in misinformation. They also face difficulties in speaking effectively and efficiently about human rights issues in the international and domestic arenas, where political and cultural dynamics are constantly changing. [10]

The lack of political and financial support from local and international governments is also a major challenge for diplomats in their ongoing efforts to support and protect human rights. Without sufficient political and diplomatic support, they may locate themselves in a weak position, unable to exert effective influence. [11] Facing these challenges requires diplomats to have excellent negotiation and persuasion skills and to be able to handle pressure, as well as to maintain diplomatic ethics and values in their actions. Such an endeavour requires a strong spirit and a willingness to face challenges with determination and confidence.

The reciprocal influence between domestic policy and diplomacy

The reciprocal influence between domestic policy and diplomacy is a complex issue that deserves deep thought and careful analysis. States' domestic policies heavily influence diplomacy, and diplomatic relations with other states also greatly influence domestic policy. [12] If we look at the relationship between domestic policy and diplomacy from a human rights perspective, we find that there is a mutual influence between the two that can affect the fate of rights and freedoms in states. [13]

The domestic politics of states must be studied carefully to understand how diplomacy can be effective in protecting human rights, as diplomatic decisions are often a direct result of states' domestic policies. On the other hand, international relations and diplomacy can also influence the formulation of domestic policies, including international pressure to respect human rights and improve domestic policies in this regard. [14]

Diplomacy can therefore be an effective mechanism for transferring international pressure and scrutiny to the domestic policies of states with the aim of improving and ensuring respect for human rights. [15] This highlights the role of domestic policy and diplomacy in building a strong partnership for the defence of human rights and the need to understand this mutual influence to ensure that humanitarian objectives are achieved in domestic policies and diplomatic decisions.

The effectiveness of human rights organisations as partners in diplomacy

Human rights organisations are an essential part of

the international human rights protection system, monitoring and assessing the situation and reporting on human rights violations in different countries. [16] In addition, these organisations intervene and mediate with governments and relevant authorities to correct situations and protect victims. These organisations are important partners for diplomats in achieving justice and enforcing human rights on the ground.

Diplomats should work in coordination and cooperation with these organisations to ensure the protection of human rights at the national and international levels. Part of the role of human rights organisations as diplomatic partners is to lobby and influence states and the international community to enact legislation and resolutions that protect and promote human rights. [17]

Their role is not limited to monitoring and reporting but also includes providing expertise and guidance to diplomats to achieve human rights goals on the ground. It is essential to emphasise the importance of integrating the efforts of human rights organisations with those of diplomats to ensure that human rights are respected and enforced throughout the world.

Assessing diplomacy as an effective mechanism for defending rights

The study and analyses presented in this research show that diplomacy is a very effective mechanism for supporting and defending human rights. In light of the significant challenges facing the international community, diplomacy can play a prominent role in promoting and protecting human rights. The multitude of issues raised by international organisations in the context of human rights highlights the importance of a diplomatic approach in dealing with these issues in a coherent and effective manner, which emphasises the role of diplomacy as one of the main tools in shaping global human rights policies. It must be emphasised that achieving human rights is not easy, and diplomatic efforts often face severe challenges that need to be addressed with wisdom and patience.

Nevertheless, diplomacy remains vital in providing solutions and recommendations that contribute to realising human rights interests. In this context, it is also critical to recognise the impact of cultural and social contexts on the understanding and interpretation of human rights, which calls for a multi-directional and diverse diplomatic approach to ensure the coherence of international human rights principles. Therefore, it can be said with confidence that diplomacy bears a significant responsibility in placing human rights on the global agenda and making the necessary efforts to ensure that these rights are realised on the ground.

References

Diplomacy as a Tool for Defending Human Rights

[1] Al-Mansouri, Fatima. The Impact of Bilateral Cooperation on Basic Human Rights. Cairo: Rights Publication, 2019.

[2] Smith, John. International Cooperation in Human Rights: Strategies for Enhancing Basic Rights. New York: Human Rights Press, 2020.

[3] Brandon J. Kinne. 'Network Dynamics and the Evolution of International Cooperation.' *American Political Science Review*, 107 (2013): 766 - 785. https://doi.org/10.1017/S0003055413000440

[4] C. Bodea and Fangjin Ye. 'Investor Rights versus Human Rights: Do Bilateral Investment Treaties Tilt the Scale?' *British Journal of Political Science*, 50 (2018): 955–977.

https://doi.org/10.1017/S0007123418000042

[5] Johnson, Emily. International Treaties and Human Rights: A Comprehensive Overview. London: Global Rights Publishing, 2021.

[6] Abu Zaid, Omar. Human Rights Agreements: Their Impact and Implementation. Beirut: Middle Eastern Studies Press, 2018.

[7] Lane, Lottie. "Mitigating Humanitarian Crises during Non-International Armed Conflicts—the Role of Human Rights and Ceasefire Agreements." Journal of International Humanitarian Action 1 (2016).

[8] Human rights issues greatly influenced South Africa's diplomatic relations during and after apartheid, leading to the transition from an oppressive regime to a democratic one and increased American support. See:

Naeli Fitria. "Exploring the Impact of Human Rights on Diplomatic Relations: A Comparative Analysis of State Interactions." COMSERVA : *Jurnal Penelitian dan Pengabdian Masyarakat* (2023). https://doi.org/10.59141/comserva.v3i1.755.

[9] The European Union cooperates with BRICS countries on human rights issues, but pursuing common goals remains challenging due to differing political structures and understandings of human rights protection.

Francisca Costa Reis, Weiyuan Gao and Vineet Hegde. 'The EU's engagement with foreign powers on human rights.' *The European Union and Human Rights* (2020).

https://doi.org/10.1093/OSO/9780198814191.003.0013.

[10] Bakke, Kristin M., Neil J. Mitchell, and Hannah M. Smidt. 2019. Source cited.

[11] Alston, Philip. (2017). Cited source.

[12] Putnam, R. "Diplomacy and Domestic Politics: The Logic of Two-Level Games." International Organisation 42 (1988): 427–60.

[13] Jamie J. Gruffydd-Jones. 'Citizens and Condemnation: Strategic Uses of International Human Rights Pressure in Authoritarian States.' Comparative Political Studies, 52 (2018): 579 - 612. https://doi.org/10.1177/0010414018784066.

[14] Some believe that Britain's exit from the European Union could lead to significant gaps in Britain's international human rights diplomacy, unless addressed. See:

Rhona K. M. Smith, Conall Mallory and Seán Molloy. 'Brexiting human rights diplomacy at the United Nations Human Rights Council: opportunity or cause for concern?' The International Journal of Human Rights, 24 (2020): 414–438. https://doi.org/10.1080/13642987.2019.1645130.

[15] Dasandi, N. "Foreign Aid Donors, Domestic Actors, and Human Rights Violations: The Politics and Diplomacy of Opposing Uganda's Anti-Homosexuality Act." Journal of International Relations and Development 25 (2022): 657–84.

[16] NGOs can provide valuable information and recommendations to diplomats and policymakers on human rights issues. See:

Zhang, Dechun, and Ahmed Bux Jamali. "China's 'Weaponised' Vaccine: Intertwining Between International and Domestic Politics." East Asia 39 (2022): 279–96.

[17] Key strategies used by human rights NGOs include "naming and shaming" human rights violators, advocacy, information sharing, and cooperation with governments. See:

Murdie, Amanda, D. R. Davis, and Baekkwan Park. "Advocacy Output: Automated Coding Documents from Human Rights Organisations." Journal of Human Rights 19 (2020): 83–98.

6
International Organisations
And the Shaping of Human Rights Standards

The importance of international organisations in human rights governance

International organisations are an important platform for promoting and protecting human rights on a global scale. They work to develop and adopt standards and laws, monitor compliance with them, and provide support and assistance to states in promoting human rights within their borders. The role of international organisations is fundamental in promoting awareness of human rights and the need to respect them at all times and in all circumstances.

The existence of these organisations contributes to spreading a culture of human rights and deepening international understanding of them. Joint action between states and these organisations also contributes to finding comprehensive and sustainable solutions to human rights issues that may pose international challenges.

Furthermore, documenting and disseminating information and reports on human rights violations plays a crucial role in improving conditions and holding those responsible to account. Through joint efforts with states, international organisations gain a strong voice that serves to defend human rights in all their forms. Thanks to continuous interaction and cooperation between these organisations and states, significant progress can be made in the field of human rights governance at the international level.

Historical frameworks for international organisations' involvement in human rights

International organisations began their large-scale interventions in the field of human rights in the aftermath of World War II, when they realised the urgent need to protect people from the massacres and widespread violations that the world had witnessed during this bloody war. At this turning point, international organisations began to form an international legal framework to protect human rights and promote the values of justice and humanity.

Following the 1948 United Nations Declaration of Universal Human Rights, international organisations began working on drafting a charter that would guarantee the protection of human rights at the global level. This period marked the beginning of the development of international organisations' involvement in the field of human rights and the establishment of a legal framework to ensure respect for and consolidation of these rights. Subsequently, the international community issued numerous conventions and treaties to safeguard human rights and address the horrific violations suffered by peoples and individuals. [1]

The influence of these organisations on the international stage also grew, as they began to play a key role in mobilising international public opinion and influencing national and global policies on human rights. [2] Over time, these organisations grew in power and influence, gaining broader powers to monitor respect for human rights and intervene in international conflicts with the aim of protecting civilians and achieving humanitarian justice. In this context, the historical frameworks for international organisations' intervention in the field of human rights are important as a necessary reference for understanding current debates on the role of these organisations and guiding future efforts towards promoting and protecting human rights at the international and regional levels.

The United Nations plays a leading role in establishing international human rights standards

The United Nations is known for its leading role in formulating and developing international human rights standards, playing a central role in coordinating global efforts to emphasise the importance of respecting and promoting human rights. The United Nations was founded with the aim of promoting international cooperation, world peace and human rights, and the formulation of the United Nations Charter, which defines human rights and freedoms, was one of its main objectives. The United Nations has set up a number of programs and systems to protect and promote human rights around the world in response to the problems of the modern world. [3]

One of the most notable of these initiatives was the establishment of the Office of the United Nations High Commissioner for Human Rights, which monitors respect for human rights and provides recommendations and guidance to states to improve their human rights performance. The United Nations has also adopted several international human rights conventions and encouraged member states to ensure their respect and implementation.

In addition, the United Nations plays an important role in providing technical and financial support to developing countries to strengthen their human rights capacities. It is worth noting that the United Nations works to promote a culture of human rights and raise awareness through its educational and awareness programmes. Embodying a pioneering spirit in the field of human rights, the United Nations remains a vital partner in developing and promoting international human rights standards, nurturing their achievements, and achieving justice and equality for all peoples of the world.

The International Criminal Court's efforts to promote human justice

The International Criminal Court (ICC) is one of the most important international organisations, established to promote humanitarian justice and combat crimes against humanity. The court was established as a means of holding individuals accountable for war crimes and crimes against humanity [4] and also aims to promote international peace and security through the application of the principles of justice.

Since its establishment, the ICC has persistently engaged in efforts to combat impunity for war crimes and crimes against humanity. [6] The Court also seeks to promote respect for human rights and the application of international justice as a key mechanism for achieving international peace and security. [7] The ICC's efforts to promote human justice are essential and vital in light of the challenges and threats facing the world today. Many recent international conflicts and wars have revealed serious human rights abuses and war crimes, and this is where the ICC plays a role in providing a means of delivering justice and restoring rights that have been taken away.

The Court works through cases involving specific individuals and the analysis of evidence and testimony to achieve justice and hold those involved in serious human rights violations and war crimes accountable.

Thus, the role of the International Criminal Court in promoting human justice is fundamental to building a more equitable and peaceful future for humanity.

Cooperation between regional and global organisations for sustainable formulation

Cooperation between regional and global organisations is vital to formulating sustainable human rights standards. Regional organisations represent direct efforts that control local issues and the details of culture and history in different regions, while global organisations add comprehensive experience and general insights into humanitarian issues. This cooperation aims to strike a balance between the global and local dimensions of human rights and reflects the spirit of international cooperation in the pursuit of justice and equality. [8]

Cooperation between these organisations helps to ensure an effective response to human rights challenges at the regional and global levels, thereby promoting shared responsibility and complementarity in addressing human rights issues. [9] In addition, this cooperation can raise awareness about the importance of protecting human rights and contribute to strengthening the capacity of regional organisations to adopt global standards and implement them in their local contexts.

It is worth noting that the challenges faced by regional and global organisations in the cooperation process include competing interests, political and economic challenges, and differences in interests and cultures. Therefore, effective cooperation between these regional and global organisations requires clear visions and joint initiatives aimed at strengthening the capacities of governments and civil society to participate in the formulation and effective implementation of standards. Consequently, such cooperation can contribute to strengthening international human rights work and building a sustainable future based on equality and justice.

Challenges of implementation: the gap between standards and reality

The challenges of implementing international human rights standards are a central focus of the international debate on how to translate standards into reality to realise human rights for all. Despite the adoption and agreement of standards by international organisations, there is a significant gap between the extent to which states adhere to these standards and the actual situation on the ground. [10] This is evident in the daily policies and actions of states and is reflected in the gap in development and economic growth, in the provision of basic services, and in the achievement of equality and justice.

The gap between standards and reality [11] shows that political, economic, and social issues have a significant impact on the application of international standards. [12] However, collective action between international organisations and the international community can reduce this gap. [13] By focusing on promoting transparency and accountability and strengthening international cooperation at all levels, we can reduce the gap between international standards and local realities. Consequently, the introduction of political pressure can contribute to guiding international organisations towards a genuine commitment to these standards and their effective and sustainable implementation on the ground.

The impact of political pressure on international organisations' policies

International organisations play a vital role in promoting and protecting human rights globally. However, it is undeniable that these organisations may face significant challenges as a result of political pressure. Political pressure can greatly influence the policies of these organisations and prevent them from achieving their specific humanitarian goals. International organisations become vulnerable to pressure from member states and relevant parties, which negatively affects the quality of their decisions and work. [14]

This pressure can influence the direction of international organisations, leading them to ignore human rights issues or make concessions to improve diplomatic relations. In fact, international organisations may face difficult situations when confronting such pressures, as they must maintain their credibility and uphold human rights values without succumbing to political pressure. [15] Hence, it becomes necessary to understand the impact of political pressure on the policies of international organisations in a deep and clear manner. [16] This requires a careful and comprehensive analysis of the political and humanitarian context, as well as the development of strategies to deal with these pressures without compromising the fundamental values and principles that international organisations protect.

Successes and failures in the application of international standards

A thorough analysis of certain cases confirms the extent to which standards have improved the human rights situation, while also revealing the difficulties and challenges facing their implementation. Reviewing successes and failures in the application of international standards is essential to understanding the role of international organisations and national efforts in promoting and protecting human rights in different regions of the world.

The analysis can reveal the successes achieved as a result of the adoption and effective implementation of standards, and highlight the failures and difficulties that can hinder the implementation of these standards. [17] By highlighting case studies, it is possible to analyse the factors that influence the success or failure of implementation and identify strengths and weaknesses in the performance of international organisations and national systems. The lessons and recommendations from these studies aim to enhance the drafting and implementation of international standards, which in turn contributes to promoting human rights and fostering positive change globally.

The role of new legislation in supporting human rights

New legislation is one of the most effective tools for promoting and protecting human rights in contemporary societies, it plays a prominent role in bringing about positive change and strengthening governments' accountability for the rights of their citizens. The importance of this legislation stems from its ability to define the limits and controls that governing authorities must adhere to in their dealings with human rights, thereby promoting justice and equality in society. Among the vital issues addressed by the new legislation are the protection of fundamental individual freedoms, such as freedom of expression and freedom of belief, and the promotion and protection of the rights of women and minorities from discrimination and persecution. This legislation also seeks to improve accountability mechanisms and provide effective protection for victims of human rights violations by introducing reliable legal mechanisms to hold perpetrators accountable and provide compensation to victims.

The role of the new legislation is particularly evident in the area of economic, social and cultural rights, where it aims to establish public policies that protect vulnerable groups and promote opportunities for participation and access to basic services. [18] This legislation also seeks to combat poverty and economic and social discrimination by enacting laws that promote the equitable distribution of wealth and guarantee citizens' rights to education, health, and adequate housing. Overall, the role of new legislation in supporting human rights is vital in light of the current challenges facing global societies [19], and governments must be careful to enact laws that reflect their genuine commitment to protecting the rights of all members of society fairly and equally.

The foreseeable future of international organisations in the field of human rights

International organisations are one of the main pillars of supporting and promoting human rights at the domestic and international levels. Despite the challenges they face, they continue to bear a significant responsibility for improving the lives of individuals and achieving equality and justice. International entitlement points to the importance of developing new policies and procedures that support human rights and highlights the future role of international organisations in this context.

The foreseeable future of international organisations in the field of human rights requires rapid and effective responses to emerging challenges and adaptations to political, social, and technological developments that affect people's lives. It is important for international organisations to stay abreast of new challenges and emerging issues that may affect human rights, and to identify priorities and urgent needs for action to promote and protect these rights. International organisations must adopt a comprehensive collaborative approach with local, regional and international stakeholders to achieve common human rights goals and bring about positive change.

It is also important to keep pace with technological developments and leverage them to promote human rights, ensuring that they are not exploited for repressive purposes. International organisations must participate in drafting legislation and policies that protect personal data and limit unlawful interference in individuals' private lives. International organisations should also focus on promoting education and awareness about human rights and defending them in line with cultural and social developments around the world. Ultimately, international organisations must take the lead in providing comprehensive and proactive solutions to future challenges affecting human rights, working in partnership with governments, civil society, and the private sector to ensure continued progress towards a more just, equitable, and dignified world for all.

References

International Organisations

[1] Gil-Bazo, María-Teresa. "Introduction: The Role of International Organisations and Human Rights Monitoring Bodies in Refugee Protection." Refugee Survey Quarterly 34 (2015): 1–10.

[2] Alfredsson, Gudmundur S., and K. Tomaševski. "A Thematic Guide to Documents on the Human Rights of Women: Global and Regional Standards Adopted by Intergovernmental Organisations, International Non-Governmental Organisations and Professional Associations." Netherlands Quarterly of Human Rights 14 (1996): 119–119.

[3] The United Nations plays a role in shaping international criminal justice by defining international law, monitoring the international community, establishing the International Court of Justice, and imposing sanctions on violators. See:

Doshie Piper and Heather Alaniz. 'United Nations Role in International Criminal Justice.' (2014): 1–5. https://doi.org/10.1002/9781118517383.WBECCJ072.

[4] The formation of the International Criminal Court has its roots in the history of previous models of judicial bodies that brought war criminals to justice and in the international discussions that surrounded its creation.

O. Huzik. 'The Genesis of the International Criminal Court.' Journal of Legal Studies, 28 (2021): 74–85. https://doi.org/10.2478/jles-2021-0012.

[5] The United Nations has played a pivotal role in the development of international criminal law through negotiations and the drafting of treaties, such as the Genocide Convention and the Rome Statute of the International Criminal Court.

See: S. Zappalà. 'International Criminal Law and UN Treaties.' *The Oxford Handbook of United Nations Treaties* (2019).

https://doi.org/10.1093/law/9780190947842.003.0027

[6] The International Criminal Court was established after the events in the former Yugoslavia and Rwanda, with a focus on punishing perpetrators of human rights violations and preventing future crimes. See:

Juma Abed FAYADH. 'THE FUNCTION OF THE INTERNATIONAL CRIMINAL COURT IN DEFENDING HUMAN RIGHTS

AGAINST CRIMES.' RIMAK *International Journal of Humanities and Social Sciences* (2023). https://doi.org/10.47832/2717-8293.22.36.

[7] The International Criminal Court has a positive impact on reducing crimes against humanity by targeting leaders who promote or tolerate such crimes, with a relatively low number of interventions.

É. Schneider, J. R. Iglesias, Karen Hallberg and M. N. Kuperman. 'Crimes against Humanity: The Role of International Courts.' *PLoS ONE*, 9 (2014). https://doi.org/10.1371/journal.pone.0099064.

[8] Multi-level cooperation between international organisations, national governments and local non-governmental organisations can initiate norm implementation processes but may not be sustainable in the long term. See, for example:

Anne Jenichen and Andrea Schapper. 'Between global ambitions and local change: how multi-level cooperation advances norm implementation in weak states.' *Journal of International Relations and Development*, 20 (2017): 1-28. https://doi.org/10.1057/JIRD.2014.29.

[9] E. Voeten. 'Competition and Complementarity between Global and Regional Human Rights Institutions.' *Global Policy*, 8 (2017): 119-123. https://doi.org/10.1111/1758-5899.12395.

[10] Medium-sized organisations implementing standards in the Better Cotton Initiative spend increasing amounts of time on data collection rather than enabling farmers to comply with the standard

through capacity building. See:

Peter Lund-Thomsen, N. Coe, Sukphal Sing and L. Riisgaard. 'Bridging Global Standard Requirements and Local Farmer Needs: Implementing Partners of the Better Cotton Initiative in Pakistan and India.' *Development and Change* (2017).

[11] Commitments in regional trade agreements (RTAs) may conflict with many sustainable development goals (SDGs), causing policy incoherence and threatening equitable access to health services. See, for example:

Arne Ruckert, Ashley Schram, R. Labonté, S. Friel, D. Gleeson and A. Thow. 'Policy coherence, health and the sustainable development goals: a health impact assessment of the Trans-Pacific Partnership.' *Critical Public Health*, 27 (2017): 86 - 96. https://doi.org/10.1080/09581596.2016.1178379.

[12] Challenges to achieving Goal 17 include a lack of political will, isolationist policies, narrow nationalism, and weak linkages between national and international rules.

Wekgari Dulume. 'Linking the SDGs with human rights: opportunities and challenges of promoting goal 17.' *Journal of Sustainable Development Law and Policy (The)* (2019). https://doi.org/10.4314/jsdlp.v10 i1.3.

[13] Tensions arise between global and regional institutions due to differences in the interpretation of rights, the judicialisation of human rights, and concerns about the impact of global institutions on re-

gional ones.

[13] Tensions arise between global and regional institutions due to differences in the interpretation of rights, the judicialisation of human rights, and concerns about rights encroaching on other areas of international cooperation.

E. Voeten. (2017). Source cited.

[14] Drubel, Julia, and Janne Mende. "The Hidden Contestation of Norms: Decent Work in the International Labour Organization and the United Nations." Global Constitutionalism, 2023.

[15] Beresford, Alexander, and D. Wand. "Understanding Bricolage in Norm Development: South Africa, the International Criminal Court, and the Contested Politics of Transitional Justice." Review of International Studies 46 (2020): 534–54.

[16] A. Naim. 'Human Rights in the Arab World: A Regional Perspective.' *Human Rights Quarterly*, 23 (2001): 701 - 732. https://doi.org/10.1353/HRQ.2001.0026.

[17] Arne Ruckert, Ashley Schram, R. Labonté, S. Friel, D. Gleeson and A. Thow. (2017). Source cited.

[18] Schulze, Meike. "The EU and the Negotiations for a Binding Treaty on Business and Human Rights," 2023.

[19] Pettoello-Mantovani, Clara. "Cybercrimes: An Emerging Category of Offences within the Frame of the International Criminal Court Jurisdiction." International Journal of Law and Politics Studies, 2024.

7
Current Challenges
Facing Human Rights Diplomats

An overview of current challenges

The world is living in a historic era in which human rights diplomacy faces increasing and complex challenges ranging from tension between national interests and international standards to the influence of domestic politics on international negotiations. Understanding these challenges is critical in the current context, where the protection of human rights depends on a delicate balance between the national interests of states and international human rights standards. The present situation requires deep reflection and comprehensive analysis to understand how to address and overcome these challenges.

Human rights diplomats must consider the impact of the media on diplomatic decision-making and provide support for international human rights standards and values. This issue is not limited to political challenges but extends to security and technological challenges, as well as cultural and religious barriers. Hence, it is important to thoroughly analyse these factors and develop effective strategies to address them.

Such an effort also requires an understanding of the ethical dilemmas that human rights diplomats may face in their pursuit of justice and the protection of human rights. Ultimately, there must be informed visions for the future that contribute to improving human rights diplomacy and successfully overcoming these challenges.

Tension exists between national interests and international standards

Human rights diplomats frequently encounter conflicts between national interests and international standards. In fact, this tension stems from the difficulty of reconciling national interests and values with international human rights standards and obligations. [1] Diplomats typically seek to defend the interests of their country or region regardless of how such desires may conflict with recognised international standards. [2]

These conflicts are particularly evident in areas such as the rights of refugees and migrants, torture and inhuman treatment, women's and minority rights, and the pursuit of social justice. Resolving this tension requires a deep understanding of the political and cultural dynamics of each country and the need to negotiate consensual solutions that balance national interests with international human rights standards. [3]

Furthermore, providing innovative and sustainable solutions requires a multidimensional strategic vision that takes into account cultural and value differences and their impact on state policies. [4] It is also important to promote dialogue and exchange of experiences between countries to achieve mutual understanding and seek consensual solutions that are in the interest of humanity. While this tension undoubtedly poses significant challenges for human rights diplomats, it may also be an area for innovation and positive progress towards achieving justice and protecting human rights in a comprehensive and equitable manner.

The media and its impact on human rights diplomacy

The media plays a vital role in shaping and defining perceptions and concepts related to human rights at the international level. It is an open window that shows what is going on in the world and brings attention to human rights violations and victories. However, the media can also reflect images in a distorted or misrepresented manner, leading to a distortion of facts or misleading the international community about the reality of the situation. [5] Promoting human rights through diplomacy requires a profound understanding of the role and influence of the media and how it shapes public opinion. [6] Diplomats should be aware of the ways in which the media can influence international relations related to human rights and how to address this influence effectively. [7]

It is important to understand how to use the media in an ethical and professional manner to promote awareness of human rights and respond to violations. Appealing to domestic and international public opinion may be necessary to ensure the success of diplomatic efforts to protect rights. In addition, diplomats should leverage the media to highlight human rights issues and challenges in a way that encourages international action and cooperation to overcome them. [8] The media has the power to attract attention and influence policy and decision-making, which can make a difference in the field of human rights by supporting international diplomacy and joint action to reach comprehensive solutions.

Ethical dilemmas for human rights diplomats

Human rights diplomats face ethical dilemmas that are fundamental to the exercise of their duties and the achievement of their goals. In their efforts to defend human rights, they face multiple ethical challenges that may influence their behaviours and decisions. One such dilemma is the balance between silence and speaking out, where diplomats may encounter themselves faced with an ethical dilemma that requires them to remain silent for the sake of diplomatic interests while at the same time feeling compelled to speak out in defence of human rights. [9] Diplomats also find themselves caught between national duty and humanitarian responsibility, sometimes having to choose between the interests of their countries and the defence of human rights around the world. [10]

Another dilemma arises in dealing with countries that violate human rights, where diplomats must engage in diplomatic work with these countries while maintaining their commitment to ethical standards and human rights, placing them in a difficult position that requires careful judgement and considerable wisdom.[11] Another ethical dilemma facing diplomats in the field of human rights is the attempt to reconcile neutrality with intervention, as they often have to act impartially, but in some circumstances they find themselves compelled to intervene to prevent human rights violations or to speak out on behalf of the voiceless.

This process requires moral flexibility and a careful assessment of complex and intertwined circumstances and interests. In this way, ethical dilemmas arise that pose a constant challenge to human rights diplomats [12], requiring them to exercise wisdom, decisiveness and balance to overcome these challenges in a way that ensures the protection of moral values and the effective defence of human rights.

The impact of domestic policies on international negotiations

The domestic policies of states have a significant impact on the conduct of international negotiations, particularly regarding human rights issues. When there are internal violations and persecution in a state, this can negatively affect that state's willingness to adhere to international human rights standards during international negotiations. [13] Hence, the main challenge for human rights diplomats is to convince states of the need to improve their own human rights records to build trust and bridges for dialogue in international negotiations.

These efforts require flexibility, diplomatic savvy, and an understanding of the political and cultural dynamics of each individual state. However, domestic issues remain the focus of diplomats, who must strike a balance between demands for human rights improvements and interference in the internal affairs of states. [14] This challenge is one of the most complex facing human rights diplomats and requires creative solutions and comprehensive international cooperation to overcome.

Security challenges and their impact on the protection of human rights

Ensuring and maintaining security is one of the most significant challenges facing human rights diplomats today. It is well known that insecurity leads to instability and disrupts efforts to protect human rights. The impact of security challenges on societies is negative at all levels and can lead to direct or indirect human rights violations. One of the most significant challenges is balancing the protection of national security and human rights. [15]

When the use of international force exceeds international boundaries, the protection of human rights becomes a difficult challenge. Coercive security measures may violate human rights and freedoms and restrict the activities of human rights defenders and non-governmental organisations, thereby weakening their role in protecting and raising awareness of those rights. [16]

Addressing these challenges requires the adoption of sophisticated diplomatic strategies that work to limit security crises and avoid military escalation that could lead to widespread human rights violations. It is also necessary to strengthen international cooperation and reinforce international legal systems relating to human rights and the ethics of the use of international force. The role of security challenges in promoting human rights cannot be ignored. From this perspective, human rights diplomats must be aware of the delicate balance between security and human rights and adopt policies and measures that effectively achieve it.

The role of technology in monitoring and promoting human rights

Technology is one of the most important factors to monitor and understand its impact on human rights in the current era. Technological advancements have led to the development of surveillance and espionage methods, potentially violating individuals' privacy and rights. However, technology can also be used to promote and defend human rights. We can use social media and the internet as tools to raise awareness of human rights and promote positive social change.

Furthermore, technology is used to collect data and statistics to understand the extent of human rights violations and develop effective solutions. Nevertheless, the use of technology must be monitored carefully, and its impact on human rights understood.[17]

It is necessary to develop policies and laws that regulate the use of technology in relation to human rights and ensure transparency and accountability with regard to data collection and use. [18] Awareness of the ethics of technology use and its impact on human rights must be promoted through education and training, and individuals' rights to protection from technological surveillance and privacy violations must be guaranteed. Striking a balance between benefiting from technology on the one hand and preserving human rights and privacy on the other is an important challenge that must be addressed in the modern digital age.

Cultural and religious barriers

Cultural and religious barriers are major hurdles for human rights diplomats in their efforts to promote and protect human rights at the international and national levels. Cultural differences between countries and societies contribute to cultural diversity, but they can also lead to clashes and conflicts in the understanding and application of basic human rights concepts. [19]

Regarding religious obstacles, conflicts may arise between religious concepts and international human rights standards, making it difficult to reach a unified international agreement. Overcoming these obstacles requires a profound understanding of different cultures and religions and the building of bridges of communication and understanding between nations and communities. Constructive international dialogue based on respect and appreciation of differences must also be encouraged by promoting and reinforcing the values of openness and tolerance. [20]

Furthermore, diplomats and human rights negotiators must work to raise awareness of the importance of human rights in a manner that respects cultural and religious diversity and highlights the fundamental values shared by different cultures and religions. To overcome cultural and religious barriers to human rights, avenues for international cooperation should be explored, and the exchange of experiences and knowledge between different cultures should be encouraged. We should also promote awareness of human rights and their importance in a manner that aligns with the context of each culture and religion. Cooperation and understanding across cultural and religious boundaries can contribute to comprehensive and sustainable solutions for realising human rights around the world.

Strategies for dealing with international pressure

The challenges posed by international pressure on human rights diplomats cannot be ignored. In the arena of international diplomacy, human rights diplomacy may face multiple and varied pressures, ranging from political to economic to cultural. [21] These pressures require diplomats in this field to employ careful tactics and strategies to confront them. Diplomats need to carefully consider several aspects of their strategies for dealing with international pressures.

Firstly, diplomats need to comprehend the diverse national and international perspectives and interests that impact the human rights domain. They must be able to make informed and calculated decisions that balance their country's interests with international obligations.

Second, diplomats should adopt a strategy of building strong international alliances that support human rights issues. These alliances will play a major role in promoting international positions and demands and providing support for human rights demands in international forums. In the same vein, diplomats must have the ability to negotiate internationally and draft agreements and treaties that promote and protect human rights. Negotiations in this context must be subject to standards of integrity, transparency, and credibility.

Finally, diplomats must have a long-term strategic vision aimed at achieving radical change in international positions and policies towards human rights. They must work to encourage international organisations and diplomats to update and develop international legal frameworks to achieve greater human rights protection and more effective implementation.

Visions for the Future of Human Rights Diplomacy

In concluding this chapter, it is worth reflecting on the future of human rights diplomacy and the challenges it may face. It is important to understand that political, social, and technological developments will pose new challenges that require a wise and sustainable diplomatic response. It is becoming necessary to seek mechanisms to promote and protect human rights in the face of rapid and complex changes in global societies.

The main dilemma remains how to balance national interests with international human rights standards. In the coming years, diplomats will play a crucial role in ensuring that these challenges and needs are met while preserving human values and principles. Promoting international understanding and cooperation in the field of human rights is one of the most important pillars for ensuring the prosperity of peoples and nations. We must seek ways to strengthen partnerships among governments, international organisations and civil society with the aim of promoting and protecting human rights globally.

We must also encourage the positive use of technology to enhance human rights monitoring and address violations, without succumbing to the negative uses of technology in privacy violations and illegal espionage.

We should also encourage constructive intercultural and interfaith dialogue to overcome cultural and religious barriers that may hinder efforts to promote human rights.

Finally, we must recognise that achieving positive change requires joint efforts from all stakeholders, which calls for structural and tactical reforms in the context of human rights diplomacy. The future of human rights diplomacy depends on our ability to adapt and innovate to meet challenges and contribute to progress and change towards a more just and humane world.

References

Current Challenges

[1] In the following article, the author explores the tension between promoting the national interest and focusing on international ethical obligations in diplomacy:

B. Barder. 'Diplomacy, Ethics and the National Interest: What Are Diplomats For?' *The Hague Journal of Diplomacy*, 5 (2010): 289-297. https://doi.org/10.1163/187119110X511653.

[2] Sulyok, Márton. "Compromise(d)? – Perspectives of Rule of Law in the European Union," 2:207–27, 2021.

[3] Behrens argues that applying general principles of harmonisation can help diplomats overcome the tension between national interests and international standards in human rights cases.

Paul Behrens. '"None of Their Business"? Diplomatic Involvement in Human Rights.' *Melbourne Journal of*

International Law, 15 (2014): 190-227.

[4] Wan, M. "International Humanitarian Law and the US-China Rivalry: National Interests and Human Rights Linkage." Asian Perspective 46 (2022): 605–25.

[5] Authoritarian regimes may use international human rights pressure to bolster their domestic support, by shifting attention to defending the nation rather than focusing on individual violations. See, for example:

Jamie J. Gruffydd-Jones. 'Citizens and Condemnation: Strategic Uses of International Human Rights Pressure in Authoritarian States.' *Comparative Political Studies*, 52 (2018): 579 - 612. https://doi.org/10.1177/0010414018784066.

[6] Bullion, S. J. "Press Roles in Foreign Policy Reporting." Gazette 32 (1983): 179–88.

[7] Soltanipour, Samane, and Akbar Nasrollahi. "Media Impartiality and Its Impact on the Observance of Human Rights in the Media." Bioethics 9 (2019): 139–57.

[8] R. Mullerson. 'Human Rights Diplomacy.' (1997). https://doi.org/10.4324/9781315005188.

[9] Anupama Ghosal and Sreeja Pal. (2020): Source cited.

[10] Witt, H., and Karyn Levin. "Ethical Dilemmas in Human Rights Field Education: A Case Study on Macro Practice in a Reproductive-Rights Policy Setting." Journal of Human Rights and Social Work 6 (2020): 78–81.

[11] C. H. Wellman. 'Debate: Taking Human Rights Seriously*.' *Journal of Po-

litical Philosophy, 20 (2012): 119-130. https://doi.org/10.1111/J.1467-9760.2011.00407.X.

[12] González, Pedro Arcos, and Rick Kye Gan. "The Evolution of Humanitarian Aid in Disasters: Ethical Implications and Future Challenges." Philosophies, 2024.

[13] Putnam, R. (1988): Source cited.

[14] Friedrichs, Gordon M. "Conceptualising the Effects of Polarisation for US Foreign Policy Behaviour in International Negotiations: Revisiting the Two-Level Game." International Studies Review, 2022.

[15] Nandy, Debasish. "Human Rights in the Era of Surveillance: Balancing Security and Privacy Concerns." Journal of Current Social and Political Issues, 2023.

[16] Karpachova, N. "Modern Challenges to International Security and Protection of Human Rights (International and Ukrainian Context)." JOURNAL OF THE NATIONAL ACADEMY OF LEGAL SCIENCES OF UKRAINE, 2021.

[17] Uhanova, N. "Challenges and Threats to the Human Rights and Safety in an Information Sphere." INFORMATION AND LAW, 2018.

[18] This paper discusses data protection laws and their impact on consumer rights in the digital economy:

Prastyanti, R. A., and Ridhima Sharma. "Establishing Consumer Trust Through Data Protection Law as a Competitive Advantage in Indonesia and India." Journal of Human Rights Culture and Legal System, 2024.

[19] This article discusses the tension between local cultural contexts and global standards in social work: Meng, Qian, M. Gray, Lieve Bradt, and G. Roets. "A Critical Review of Chinese and International Social Work: Walking a Tightrope between Local and Global Standards." International Social Work 65 (2021): 1301–13.

[20] The call to promote the values of openness and tolerance cannot be one-sided. It is unreasonable for some to understand that this requirement concerns only Islamic countries; it also concerns non-Islamic countries, especially when they do not restrain the far-right movements that are active in them—in the name of democracy and human rights—with freedom and legal protection, while their discourse is full of hatred and incitement against Muslims. See our recently published book in this regard:

Hichem Karoui. Breaking the Veil: Unmasking Stigma Against Islam in the West. Global East-West. (London: 2024).

[21] Sidhu, Jatswan S. "Human Rights Violations in Myanmar and the Military Junta's Defensive Human Rights Diplomacy." Journal of International Students, 2020.

8
National Sovereignty Versus Human Rights
An Impossible Balance?

Definition of sovereignty and human rights

National sovereignty and human rights are among the concepts that have most occupied the minds of philosophers, diplomats and thinkers throughout the ages. Sovereignty represents a state's complete control over its territory and people and is a fundamental principle in the system of international relations and internal power structures. Human rights, on the other hand, are the basic principles and values that a state must protect and guarantee for its citizens without discrimination or violation.

Historically, the concepts of national sovereignty and human rights have been intertwined in an arena of conflict and contradiction. In many cases, the principles of national sovereignty have been used as a pretext for human rights violations, leading to significant tensions between states and the international community. Establishing a clear conceptual framework for the fundamental principles related to sovereignty and human rights is urgently needed to understand the depth of this contradiction and to strive for a balance between national immunity and the protection of human rights.

Theoretical frameworks of national sovereignty and human rights

The great diversity of cultures and values around the world has given rise to multiple theoretical frameworks that explore the balance between national sovereignty and human rights from different perspectives. Classical diplomatic doctrines stipulate that state sovereignty is a fundamental principle that must be respected, whereby a state's decision is considered binding and not subject to external interference. [1]

However, in these contexts, the concept of human rights is understood as follows: if the interests of the state conflict with human rights, the interests of the state must take precedence over human rights. In contrast, modern theoretical schools emphasise the importance of preserving human rights as an essential part of political and social development. These theoretical frameworks seek to make sovereignty and human rights not contradictory, but rather an integral part of diplomatic theory and practice. [2]

Recognising the values of sovereignty regardless of circumstances and protecting human rights at all times and in all circumstances is a challenge worthy of every state and every international organisation. [3] This issue necessarily leads to competing approaches to diplomacy in this regard, as theoretical frameworks need to re-examine the relationship between sovereignty and human rights in line with the current reality. [4] This highlights the importance of specific theoretical frameworks that generate discussion on how to achieve the optimal balance between state sovereignty and commitment to human rights.

The diplomatic history of the conflict between sovereignty and human rights

The conflict between the concept of national sovereignty and human rights dates back many centuries in the history of international relations. Many civilisations and empires have witnessed bloody conflicts between ruling powers and citizens or colonised peoples. With the development of international relations and the emergence of modern diplomatic systems, these conflicts have become more complex and taken on new forms.

The concepts of national sovereignty and human rights began to clash in the arena of global politics and their impact on peoples and nations during times of world wars and popular uprisings. This conflict was accompanied by the development of political, legal and ethical ideas about human rights [5] and the exchange of views and positions between states and world powers. International conflicts have also witnessed many historical events that have entrenched issues and controversies related to the balance between sovereignty and human rights and their impact on international relations and interactions between states and the international community. [6]

Analysing the diplomatic history of this conflict is crucial to understanding the political and legal transformations that human societies have undergone throughout the ages, as well as to guiding the practical application of the concepts of sovereignty and human rights in the modern era.

Analysis of models of states that have successfully combined sovereignty and human rights

Over the decades, we have seen rare examples of states that have been able to combine the principles of national sovereignty and human rights in a tangible and successful manner. Examples of such states include the Scandinavian countries of Sweden and Norway, each of which has managed to build a strong democracy that preserves its national sovereignty while protecting and respecting human rights.

Their historical journey has been marked by many challenges and conflicts, but they have managed to refine a unique model based on balance and harmony between sovereignty and human rights. The experience of other European countries, such as Germany and the Netherlands, which have successfully adopted political systems that respect the fundamental rights of citizens while achieving their economic and political goals, can also be drawn upon. These models are important for understanding how to reconcile state sovereignty with respect for human rights, in terms of lessons that can be learnt from building other models around the world that achieve balance and social justice.

Controversial cases around the world

A study of controversial cases around the world reveals significant contradictions and challenges in reconciling the concept of national sovereignty with human rights. Historically, political systems around the world have witnessed many controversial conflicts between human rights and the concept of sovereignty. Perhaps the most prominent example of this is the way some countries deal with issues of individual freedoms and minority rights. [7] The excessive use of force and restrictions on individual freedoms are central issues that challenge the balance between sovereignty and human rights. Some cases in history have seen excessive use of force without respect for human rights, leading to atrocities and abuses of national sovereignty. [8]

In addition, the way some states deal with minority issues and rights raises questions about the discriminatory and exclusionary use of national power, reflecting a conflict between preserving national sovereignty and guaranteeing minority rights. Controversial cases underscore that reconciling the concept of sovereignty with human rights remains a major challenge in a changing and volatile world.

The study of controversial cases highlights the importance and necessity of adapting the traditional concept of sovereignty to a broader concept that takes human rights into account. Legislative frameworks must be developed to provide effective protection for human rights and ensure a balance between national sovereignty and human rights. This requires a spirit of international cooperation and a commitment by all parties to achieve justice, equality and freedom for all.

Criticisms of the concept of sovereignty in relation to human rights

The concept of sovereignty and its role in relation to human rights raises much criticism and controversy in international circles. Some consider that the traditional concept of sovereignty represents a major obstacle to the realisation and respect of human rights in the contemporary world. They attribute this criticism to the political use of sovereignty to suppress freedoms and violate human rights, especially in countries with dictatorial or authoritarian political systems. [9]

They consider that the concept of sovereignty grants states excessive and unrestricted powers over their people, which can be misused to suppress freedoms and violate human rights. It is difficult to ignore these criticisms, especially in light of events in some countries around the world that highlight the extent to which some sovereign regimes deviate from the realisation and respect of human rights.

It is necessary to consider developing the concept of sovereignty and defining its limits so that it is compatible with respecting and promoting human rights. Herein lies the challenge: how can a balance be achieved between the rights of sovereign states and human rights? Can the system of sovereignty be reformulated in a way that is compatible with the realisation and respect of human rights without the state losing its sovereignty and independence? This is a pressing and weighty challenge that requires deep reflection and great responsibility on the part of leaders and decision-makers in the international community.

The impact of globalisation on state sovereignty and human rights

Globalisation is one of the most significant phenomena that has posed a major challenge to the balance between sovereignty and human rights in the modern era. Our contemporary world has witnessed a tremendous increase in trade, technology, culture and politics between states and peoples, leading to social and economic convergence and interaction between different regions and cultures. With this development, national borders have become less clearly defined, and the impact of national and international decisions and events has diminished significantly.[10]

While we are witnessing an increase in global interconnectedness and the identification of common global interests, this development raises fundamental questions about how globalisation affects state sovereignty and human rights. On the one hand, economic, cultural and political interdependence between states may lead to mutual benefits and a balance that promotes democratic governance and respect for human rights.

On the other hand, globalisation may lead to new challenges that threaten state sovereignty and undermine human rights, such as economic exploitation or intellectual colonisation aimed at eliminating cultural and political diversity. [11] Previous experiences have shown that globalisation is not necessarily always a positive phenomenon. Its effects must be carefully examined, and the balance needed to preserve state sovereignty and human rights must be recognised. It is therefore important to understand and identify the potential positive and negative effects of globalisation on sovereignty and human rights [12], as this will be one of the fundamental bases for formulating future diplomatic strategies and promoting human rights at the national and international levels.

The roles of international bodies in striking a balance

International bodies play a crucial role in striking a balance between state sovereignty and human rights. Organisations such as the United Nations and Amnesty International have a significant influence on how states treat human rights issues. The United Nations and international diplomatic forums serve as a platform for discussing human rights issues and emphasising their importance, while providing guidance and recommendations to member states on respecting and promoting human rights.

These organisations also monitor and report human rights violations and impose sanctions on states that violate these rights. Through these measures, international bodies seek to strike a balance between state sovereignty and the protection of human rights. However, these bodies continue to face significant challenges in achieving their goals, such as political resistance from some states and financial and operational difficulties in implementing decisions. [13]

In addition, there may be threats to the authority of international bodies from some parties opposed to their interference in state affairs. Therefore, international bodies must act with caution and wisdom to strike a balance between state sovereignty and human rights and ensure the protection of the latter without compromising state sovereignty. [14]

Future challenges for diplomacy and human rights

The current period is witnessing enormous challenges for human rights diplomacy, as tension increases between the concept of national sovereignty and the need to respect human rights. Striking a balance between these two concepts is one of the most difficult challenges facing the international community today. [15] With advances in technology and increasing economic and cultural integration between states, it is becoming necessary to find new strategies that promote human rights without compromising national sovereignty.

One of the most prominent future challenges is the growing impact of technology on human rights. Technological advancements provide new opportunities to promote human rights and facilitate community participation, but they also raise concerns about privacy protection and government control over personal data. Other challenges include increasing isolationism and nationalism in some countries, which could negatively impact international cooperation to protect human rights globally.

Climate change and environmental degradation also pose significant challenges to human rights, particularly in poor regions. It is essential that diplomats and international leaders have a forward-looking vision that effectively addresses these challenges. International cooperation must be strengthened and strategic partnerships built to ensure respect for human rights without compromising national sovereignty. It is also necessary to stimulate scientific research and technological development that promotes human rights and meets the needs of different countries.

It is also necessary to activate the role of international organisations and civil society in monitoring respect for human rights and lobbying for positive change. Addressing future challenges in diplomacy and human rights requires joint efforts and a deep understanding of the complex interaction between the interests of states and human rights. As we look to the future, we must always remember that protecting human rights benefits all of humanity and promotes global stability and economic and social progress.

Can a new future for sovereignty and human rights be envisioned?

If future challenges require a rethinking of the relationship between sovereignty and human rights, then envisioning a new future becomes essential. The world appears to be moving towards radical changes in our understanding of national sovereignty and human rights and how they balance each other. Diplomatic and human rights issues have undergone significant transformations in recent decades, and this reality cannot be ignored. This has necessitated a search for innovative solutions that promote a balance between sovereignty and human rights.

Diplomats and decision-makers must seek new, well-considered mechanisms to deal with and radically overcome future conflicts. In this context, increasing the transparency and accountability of states and international organisations may be an important step towards building a new future in which the balance between sovereignty and human rights is stable and sustainable. The path to radical change is unlikely to be easy, as major transformations require joint effort, international cooperation, and open dialogue on complex and interrelated issues.

Meeting future challenges with flexibility and wisdom will be essential to ensuring global stability and progress. In the face of the challenges of globalisation, technology, and political and economic changes, international laws and human rights standards must be flexible and adaptable to effectively keep pace with these transformations. Only through innovation and joint cooperation can we be confident that we will successfully overcome these challenges and give future generations a bright and sustainable future.

References

National Sovereignty Versus Human Rights

[1] The researcher distinguishes between nationalist and democratic sovereign positions, highlighting the importance of local context, interpretation, and vernacular language for the sovereignty of self-governing peoples and human rights. See:

S. Benhabib. 'Claiming Rights across Borders: International Human Rights and Democratic Sovereignty.' *American Political Science Review*, 103 (2009): 691 - 704. https://doi.org/10.1017/S0003055409990244.

[2] This researcher believes that the Westphalian model of the sovereign state, based on self-government, territory, mutual recognition, and control, constitutes a standard for assessing the erosion of sovereignty in the contemporary world. See:

Stephen D. Krasner. 'Rethinking the sovereign state model.' *Review of International Studies*, 27 (2001):

17–42. https://doi.org/10.1017/S0260210501008014.

[3] This researcher argues that sovereignty and human rights are two interrelated normative elements of a single modern discourse on the legitimate state and the legitimate action of the state, which shaped the international system during the 20th century. See:

Christian Reus-Smit. 'Human rights and the social construction of sovereignty.' *Review of International Studies*, 27 (2001): 519–538. https://doi.org/10.1017/S0260210501005198.

[4] Some scholars note that newer and less stable governments tend to accept international human rights obligations to promote internal democracy and reduce political uncertainty. See:

A. Moravcsik. 'The Origins of Human Rights Regimes: Democratic Delegation in Postwar Europe.' *International Organization*, 54 (2000): 217–252. https://doi.org/10.1162/002081800551163.

[5] Some observe that national sovereignty is gradually changing under international human rights pressures, with non-governmental networks playing a key role in this transformation. See:

Kathryn Sikkink. 'Human rights, principled issue-networks, and sovereignty in Latin America.' International Organization, 47 (1993): 411–441. https://doi.org/10.1017/S0020818300028010

[6] Daniel Levy and N. Sznaider. 'Sovereignty transformed: a sociology of human rights.' *The British Journal of Sociology*, 57 4 (2006): 657–76. https://doi.org/10.1111/J.1468-4446.2006.00130.X

[7] It is worth noting that the United States, which has made itself the 'champion of human rights' abroad, along with a number of Western countries, have repeatedly turned a blind eye to the human rights of Palestinians, who have been deprived of their ancestral lands and continue to suffer the ravages of war, killing, destruction and torture at the hands of occupation soldiers, who receive full support from Western countries that reject even the idea of Palestinian resistance, despite its recognition by United Nations resolutions. This is, in fact, a moral problem. See our books:

Hichem Karoui. Children of Gaza: Requiem For a Civilisation In Decline. Global East-West (London: 2023).

----------------------- The Right To Resist. Global East-West (London: 2023).

[8] A prime example is Israel. See the two previous sources.

[9] J. Chopra and T. Weiss. 'Sovereignty Is No Longer Sacrosanct: Codifying Humanitarian Intervention.' Ethics & International Affairs, 6 (1992): 95 - 117. https://doi.org/10.1111/j.1747-7093.1992.tb00545.x

[10] Julian G. Ku and J. Yoo. 'Globalisation and Sovereignty.' Berkeley Journal of International Law, 31 (2013): 210. https://doi.org/10.15779/Z38T076.

[11] Jean Louise Cohen. 'Globalisation and Sovereignty: Rethinking Legality, Legitimacy, and Constitutionalism.' (2012). https://doi.org/10.1017/cbo9780511659041.

[12] Globalisation contributes to changing and reducing the scope of state sovereignty, which affects international agreements, financial flows, and human rights issues.

N. Sivakumar and S. Baskaran. 'Globalisation and Nation State.' *International journal for innovation education and research*, 2 (2014): 81-88. https://doi.org/10.31686/IJIER.VOL2.ISS8.225.

[13] This researcher believes that the impact of globalisation on international law must be reconsidered so that it complements universal principles such as human rights and collective security, rather than abandoning the concept of sovereignty.

Jean Louise Cohen. 'Whose Sovereignty? Empire Versus International Law.' *Ethics & International Affairs*, 18 (2004): 1 - 24. https://doi.org/10.1111/j.1747-7093.2004.tb00474.x.

[14] K. Griffin. 'Economic Globalisation and Institutions of Global Governance.' *Development and Change*, 34 (2003): 789–808. https://doi.org/10.1111/J.1467-7660.2003.00329.X.

[15] This researcher believes that sovereignty needs to be reconsidered in light of recent shifts in international relations, but that it should continue to play a central role in assessing the legitimacy or illegitimacy of global political actors. See:

O. Dahbour. 'Advocating Sovereignty in an Age of Globalisation.' *Journal of Social Philosophy*, 37 (2006): 108-126. https://doi.org/10.1111/J.1467-9833.2006.00305.X.

9
Human Rights Economics
The Mutual Impact of Economics and Rights

Defining the concept of human rights economics

The interaction between economic policies and human rights interests many researchers and critics because grasping this interaction is crucial for understanding the depth of the relationship between economic and human dimensions. This relationship has received much attention because it directly affects people's lives, communities, and global economic and social development. Therefore, it is crucial to define the concept of human rights economics and comprehend its fundamental principles and working mechanisms.

This definition aims to paint a comprehensive picture that reflects the theoretical and practical dimensions of this complex and multifaceted concept. In this context, the interaction between economic policies and the protection of human rights manifests itself in many different ways. While economic and development policies may affect an individual's standard of living and economic opportunities, they may also affect equality, social justice, and other available opportunities.

Similarly, the protection of human rights depends heavily on economic policies and the equitable distribution of wealth and opportunities. Analysing and understanding this interaction contributes to a deeper understanding of the challenges facing economic growth and the development of societies, as well as to the development of policies that promote sustainable development and the protection of human rights. As this interaction is complex and intertwined, understanding it requires a comprehensive analysis that encompasses both theoretical and practical aspects. In this context, it is necessary to clarify the most important points that demonstrate the complexity of this interaction and its impact on both individuals and societies.

The theoretical basis of the relationship between economics and human rights

The relationship between economics and human rights is a complex issue that has sparked much debate in the international arena. It represents a complex overlap between economic, social, and political aspects that affect people's lives and guide society's development. [1] The origins of this relationship can be traced back to economic, legal and ethical philosophy, where human beings are viewed as economic and social entities with rights that are no less important than their economic rights. [2]

The role of economic policies in supporting or undermining human rights

Economic policies are key to determining the extent to which human rights are supported or undermined within societies. Rulers and economic officials can significantly influence the living conditions and fundamental rights of citizens through their economic decisions. Hence, it is important to understand how economic policies can positively or negatively affect human rights. These economic policies can include decisions about the equitable distribution of income and wealth, as well as tax policies, public spending, and monetary pressure policies.

Accordingly, policies for economic growth, promoting investment, and creating secure employment opportunities are all factors that affect human rights. When decent employment opportunities are available and there is a fair distribution of income, economic and social rights are realised, and individuals' living conditions improve.

Economic policies must therefore be geared towards promoting social justice and achieving sustainable development that meets the basic needs of the most vulnerable groups in society. If economic policies lack balance and fail to consider social and human rights, they can worsen poverty and increase economic and social inequality, which negatively impacts people's fundamental rights. Hence, it is essential that economic policies be an integral part of national and international efforts to ensure the preservation and promotion of human rights in changing economic circumstances. [3]

The mutual impact of economic growth on fundamental rights

There are many ways that economic growth affects human rights. For example, long-term economic growth can raise people's standard of living and health. It can therefore contribute to the provision of adequate employment opportunities and increased income, thereby promoting economic and social human rights. However, this relationship must be viewed with caution, as economic growth may not necessarily be accompanied by an equitable distribution of wealth and opportunities in society.

An excessive focus on economic growth without attention to social justice can lead to increased economic and social disparities, negatively affecting human rights and reinforcing discrimination and injustice. Therefore, careful analysis of various economic policies and their potential impact on human rights is essential. These policies must include well-designed strategies to promote social justice and reduce disparities, as well as effective protection of human rights for all segments of society. [4]

Furthermore, we must consider the impact of global economic developments and changes in economic patterns on human rights in various societies. Rapid economic growth may contribute to the promotion of some rights, but it may also threaten others, especially in fragile environments and vulnerable communities. With this comprehensive analysis, we can avoid mistakes that may hinder progress towards sustainable justice and human rights.

Examples of how the economy impacts human rights

The topic of the impact of the economy on human rights is of considerable interest to researchers. Research shows how the economic situation in different countries can significantly affect the human rights of citizens. [5] In many countries, the effects of economic deterioration on human rights are clearly and tangibly visible.

One of the most important examples of such developments is the recent economic crisis in Greece, where unemployment has worsened and poverty has increased significantly, negatively affecting the fundamental rights of many citizens.

In developing countries, the negative effects of poverty and unemployment on human rights are even more evident, with many individuals suffering from low incomes and a lack of decent job opportunities. [6] In this context, we can draw on studies that address the situations in African countries suffering from difficult economic conditions and negative impacts on human rights, such as hunger and a lack of health and education services.

Furthermore, the effects of unequal wealth distribution on human rights can be observed in many countries, where different segments of society live below the poverty line while wealth is concentrated among a limited number of individuals [7], affecting opportunities for all and increasing discrimination and social injustice.

These examples demonstrate the close relationship between economic conditions and human rights, suggesting that one should take into account economic aspects when discussing human rights issues and developing public policies to improve economic and social conditions for all.

The economy impacts various segments of society through poverty and discrimination

Poverty and discrimination are among the biggest challenges facing societies around the world, and the poor and marginalised are particularly affected by economic decline, which has a negative impact on their lives. Difficult economic conditions increase the lack of opportunities and reduce resources for individuals and families, leading to greater social and economic divisions. If this deterioration continues without urgent and effective action, it will exacerbate discrimination and differences in living standards between different social classes. [8]

This is where social and economic policies come in to level the playing field and give everyone the same chances. Investing in improving employment opportunities and providing basic services such as education and healthcare can reduce the impact of the economy on poverty and contribute to improving the lives of marginalised groups.

To achieve this goal, decision-makers must consider implementing fair social and effective economic policies that promote inclusiveness and provide development opportunities for all members of society. On the other hand, we must avoid economic measures that widen social and economic gaps and increase the burden of poverty on vulnerable groups. Balancing economic development with the preservation of human rights is essential to building sustainable and equitable societies.

Investing in human rights: economic and social perspectives

Investing in human rights is a vital aspect that plays an

important role in building prosperous and stable societies. Investing in human rights refers to the efforts and resources allocated to ensuring the protection of fundamental rights, such as health, education, and a decent life for all members of society. [9] Effective investment in human rights requires strategies based on economic and social foundations that aim to achieve justice and sustainable development.

On the other hand, economics views investment as the process of allocating resources to achieve economic returns and benefits. This is where challenges and paradoxes arise in trying to reconcile economic goals with the realisation of human rights. [10]

The impact of investment in human rights is evident in the achievement of comprehensive development and the promotion of social stability by providing opportunities for all members of society to participate effectively in public and economic life. From this perspective, investment in human rights refers to the recognition of the importance of providing an environment conducive to social justice and equal opportunities. [11]

Investing in human rights reduces social disparities and achieves economic balance by enhancing productivity and raising living standards. In this context, economic and social policies play a vital role in balancing economic and social objectives. It also highlights the importance of adopting a comprehensive approach that focuses on equality and justice in directing investment towards improving living conditions for all without discrimination. Achieving this goal requires working to strengthen social protection frameworks and enhance the capacities of individuals through economic and social empowerment. In this way, investment in human rights becomes an integral part of achieving economic and social sustainability.

Economic competition and the arms race in human rights

For centuries, humans have exchanged resources, power and wealth to survive and prosper. This competition has evolved into a race that encompasses every aspect of life, including the economy and human rights. This race reflects how people act and think in today's world, particularly in the relationship between states and societies. [12]

This race poses a risk of neglecting human rights or using them as a tool for achieving economic and strategic gains. [13] This race is influenced by multiple factors, including technological advances, global economic shifts, state policies, and geopolitical competition. The competitive race between major economic powers has a significant impact on human rights around the world. [14] This phenomenon is clearly evident in issues related to cheap labour, climate change, children's rights, and socioeconomic discrimination.

Countries must recognise this complex reality by

implementing balanced and sustainable economic policies that consider both the human and social impacts in addition to the economic ones. The world needs an economic model based on sustainable development and the preservation of human rights as a fundamental part of its approach. Diplomacy can play a leading role in this area by promoting international cooperation and encouraging balanced economic policies that foster economic growth without compromising human rights. This approach can transform the economic race into a chance to achieve sustainable development and advance human rights for everyone.

We should propose economic policies that uphold human rights

Global studies and experiences suggest that sound and sustainable economic policies can positively impact human rights. We should gear these policies towards promoting economic equality and opportunities for all members of society, irrespective of their gender or social background. Among the proposals that can be adopted to promote human rights through economic policies are increasing investment in education and healthcare, guaranteeing a basic income for vulnerable and disadvantaged groups, and encouraging investment in infrastructure and technology to provide decent and sustainable employment opportunities.

Improvements can also be achieved by activating partnerships between the public sector, the private sector, and civil society to direct investments towards sustainable social and environmental projects. Sustainable development cannot be achieved without the activation of governments and international institutions in establishing monitoring and regulatory mechanisms to ensure the fair and balanced distribution of wealth and opportunities.

In summary, economic policies that promote human rights must embrace the principles of inclusiveness and social justice as fundamental measures of success and be an integral part of a comprehensive vision aimed at building prosperous and sustainable societies that achieve justice and progress for all.

Integrating the economy with human rights is essential for achieving a sustainable future

Integrating the economy and human rights is crucial to achieving a sustainable future that ensures prosperity for all. The respect and promotion of human rights, along with economic dynamics, significantly influence the well-being and progress of societies. [15]

Economic growth enhances access to fundamental rights, such as education, health, and adequate housing, while the realisation of human rights strengthens the economy by creating an environment conducive to investment and innovation.

The effective integration of the economy and human rights is evident in the ability of societies to achieve comprehensive and sustainable development, where economic growth is linked to social justice and equal opportunities for all members of society. We must gear economic policies towards promoting human rights and reducing economic and social disparities, with a focus on ethical and sustainability principles.

Achieving integration between the economy and human rights requires strong international cooperation and advanced visions for developing economic and social policies that strike a balance between economic growth and social justice. It also requires a commitment to strengthening international cooperation and exchanging experiences to ensure sustainable development and positive interaction between the economy and human rights. [16]

Therefore, this conclusion should be a motivation to work diligently towards creating economic models based on justice and sustainability that strike a balance between economic prosperity and respect for human rights. [17] We must work together as an international community to strive for a sustainable future that guarantees a decent life for all human beings.

Conclusion

Overall, research addresses the interrelationship between the economy and human rights and how each can influence the other. Studies in this field range from analysing the economic impact of human rights to exploring how human rights principles can be integrated into economic policies to assessing the challenges and opportunities that arise from this interaction. The above can be summarised with the following key points:

Integration between the economy and human rights:

There is a growing trend towards integrating human rights into economic policies, which can lead to improved social justice and increased freedoms and choices for individuals [18].

Human rights can provide a normative framework that helps economists address issues of exploitation and power relations. [19]

The economic impact of human rights:

Basic human rights promote investment in human and physical capital, but may not contribute significantly to improving productivity. [20]

Social or libertarian rights contribute to improving productivity but do not encourage investment in physical capital. [21]

Challenges in integrating human rights into economic policies:

There is a historical and contemporary disconnect between human rights and economic policies, which complicates the process of integrating them [22]. Some economists argue that human rights can make the legal system less efficient and that broad social rights may be incompatible with market economies. [23]

The recognition of economic, social, and cultural rights as human rights is essential:

There is an urgent need to reintegrate economic, social and cultural rights into the mainstream human rights paradigm, especially given the challenges they face in some regions.[24]

Global impacts:

Globalisation and democracy can sometimes be at odds, which affects how human rights are applied in different economic contexts. [25]

Thus, research indicates that there is a complex interaction between economics and human rights, where each can reinforce the other in some contexts while facing challenges in others. Integrating human rights into economic policies can lead to improved social justice and increased freedoms, but this requires overcoming the historical and contemporary separation between these two fields.

References

Human Rights Economics

[1] Research shows that there is complementarity between economic theories and human rights principles, as the latter can help overcome some of the shortcomings of economic welfare theory and address issues of exploitation and power relations. See :

Dan Seymour, Jonathan Pincus. (2008). Human Rights and Economics : the Conceptual Basis for their Complementarity. https://doi.org/10.1111/j.1467-7679.2008.00415.x

[2] Some research highlights the importance of transforming economic thinking to address current challenges such as extreme poverty, inequality and environmental threats, and emphasises that human rights can bring about radical change in economic

policy and planning in the interests of social justice. See, for example :

Radhika Balakrishnan, James Heintz, Diane Elson. What Does Inequality Have to Do With Human Rights? 2015. https://shorturl.at/mjtEz

[3] Some suggest that human rights economics should be a separate and complementary branch of economics, integrating fundamental principles into economic thought and policy. See:

Caroline Dommen. 'Human Rights Economics.' Human Rights Quarterly, 45 (2023): 205-238. https://doi.org/10.1353/hrq.2023.0011.

[4] According to Blume and Voigt, fundamental human rights promote efficiency and have a positive effect on investment but not on productivity, while social or libertarian rights contribute to improved productivity. See :

L. Blume et S. Voigt. 'The Economic Effects of Human Rights.' Political Economy (Topic) (2004). https://doi.org/10.1111/j.1467-6435.2007.00383.x

[5] The article examines how women in rural Bangladesh sont disproportionnellement affectées par la pauvreté, faisant face à des taux d'illettrisme plus élevés, à la malnutrition et à la discrimination dans l'emploi.

Alam, Khosrul, Ms. Binata Rani Sen, T. Islam, and Md. Farid Dewan. "Women in Rural Economy in the Light of Poverty: Bangladesh Perspective," 2015.

[6]Matsai and Raniga (2021) examined the economic stressors and coping strategies of single mothers

living in poverty in Zimbabwe, highlighting how they deal with financial hardship and social discrimination. Matsai, Vimbainashe, and T. Raniga. "ECONOMIC STRESSORS AND COPING STRATEGIES OF SINGLE MOTHERS LIVING IN POVERTY IN ZIMBABWE." Social Work, 2021.

[7] Teodorescu and Molina (2020) analysed how Roma street workers in Sweden face racialised poverty and unstable housing conditions, illustrating how marginalised groups peuvent être exclus des opportunités économiques.

Teodorescu, Dominic, and Irene Molina. "Roma Street-Workers in Uppsala: Racialised Poverty and Super Precarious Housing Conditions in Romania and Sweden." International Journal of Housing Policy 21 (2020): 401–22.

[8] Alam, Khosrul, Ms. Binata Rani Sen, T. Islam, and Md. Farid Dewan. 2015. Cited source.

[9] Marriott et al. (2023) examine how development finance institutions are meeting their human rights obligations in the field of health, arguing that current investment approaches may limit the realisation of such right.

Marriott, Anna, Anjela Taneja, and Linda Oduor-Noah. "Are Development Finance Institutions Meeting Their Human Rights Obligations in Health?" Health and Human Rights: An International Journal 25 (2023): 141–53.

[10] Omen (2023) proposed the concept of "human rights economics" as a separate branch of economics

that integrates fundamental human rights principles into economic thought and policy.

Dommen, Caroline. "Human Rights Economics." Human Rights Quarterly 45 (2023): 205–38.

[11] Obadah (2024) examined educational endowments and their role in investing in human capital from an Islamic economic perspective, showing how they peuvent contribuer à améliorer les niveaux d'éducation et à alléger le fardeau financier sur les budgets d'État.

Obadah, Ibrahim. "Educational Endowments and Their Role in Investing in Human Capital – Islamic Economic Assessment." Jordan Journal of Islamic Studies, 2024.

[12] Guasti and Koenig-Archibugi investigated whether global trade competition has led to a race to the bottom in labour standards and found no evidence of such a race to the bottom in most countries over nearly three decades.

Guasti, A., and Mathias Koenig-Archibugi. "Has Global Trade Competition Really Led to a Race to the Bottom in Labour Standards?" International Studies Quarterly, 2022.

[13] Wang (2018) argued that a country's labour rights policies depend on the labour policy decisions of its economic competitors, which may lead to un déclin en matière de protection des travailleurs en raison de la concurrence pour les investissements étrangers et les exportations.

Wang, Zhiyuan. "Economic Competition, Policy Interdependence, and Labour Rights." New Political Economy 23 (2018) : 656-73.

[14] Efrat and Yair (2023) studied public attitudes towards arms exports to human rights violators and concluded that these actions significantly increase public opposition to arms sales.

Efrat, A., and O. Yair. "Should We Sell Arms to Human Rights Violators? What the Public Thinks." Defence and Peace Economics, 2023.

[15] Bexell et al. (2023) discussed strengthening the Sustainable Development Goals through integration with human rights, calling for a more comprehensive approach to development that incorporates such principles.

Bexell, Magdalena, T. Hickmann, and Andrea Schapper. "Strengthening the Sustainable Development Goals through Integration with Human Rights." International Environmental Agreements : Politics, Law and Economics 23 (2023) : 133-39.

[16] Mesquita (2024) proposed reinterpreting human rights in the context of the climate crisis, calling for a move beyond economic expansion and unsustainable development towards a degrowth approach that is consistent with human rights within planetary boundaries.

Mesquita, Judith R. Bueno. "Reinterpreting Human Rights in the Climate Crisis: Moving beyond Economic Growth and (Un)Sustainable Development to a Future with Degrowth." Netherlands Quarterly of Human Rights 42 (2024) : 90-115.

[17] Insani et al. (2024) explored the alignment of Islamic law, human rights, and Islamic economics in empowering Muslim women, highlighting the need for a multifaceted approach to achieving gender equality and sustainable development.

Insani, Nur, Zumiyati Sanu Ibrahim, Suud Sarim Karimullah, Yavuz Gönan, and Sulastri Sulastri. "Empowering Muslim Women: Bridging Islamic Law and Human Rights with Islamic Economics." De Jure, 2024.

[18] Caroline Dommen. 2023. Source citée.

[19] D. Seymour. (2008). Source citée.

[20] L. Blume and S. Voigt. (2004). Source citée.

[21] Ibid.

[22] A. Nolan and J. P. Bohoslavsky. 'Human rights and economic policy reforms.' *The International Journal of Human Rights*, 24 (2020) : 1247-1267. https://doi.org/10.1080/13642987.2020.1823638.

[23] L. Blume and S. Voigt. (2004). Source citée.

[24] Jessie Hohmann. 'Research handbook on economic, social and cultural rights as human rights.' *Australian Journal of Human Rights*, 27 (2021): 185–187. https://doi.org/10.1080/1323238X.2021.1954141.

[25] M. Branco. 'Economics Versus Human Rights.' (2008). https://doi.org/10.4324/9780203885024.

10
Effective Diplomacy
Strategies for Promoting Human Rights

A comprehensive view of human rights diplomacy

Diplomacy is one of the main and most effective tools for promoting and protecting human rights at the international level. It is a means by which states and the international community can interact and cooperate to develop strategies and policies that contribute to establishing a sustainable culture of human rights. This function is due to its ability to influence and communicate with various international and non-governmental actors to achieve specific goals in this area.

Achieving a comprehensive vision of human rights diplomacy requires the integration and complementarity of political, legal, economic and social aspects to ensure the radical and effective protection and promotion of these rights. Understanding the comprehensive vision of human rights diplomacy is vital to understanding how to balance the interests of states and human rights and promote international cooperation. The role of diplomacy is characterised by flexibility and sustainability, as diplomatic processes require continuous and organised efforts to ensure that objectives related to the effective promotion of human rights are achieved.

Establishing human rights-related diplomatic objectives is crucial

Setting diplomatic objectives related to human rights is vital in the context of international relations and diplomatic interactions. These objectives must be specific and consistent with the values and ethical principles associated with human rights, and they must be measurable and evaluable. A diplomatic objective concerning human rights should aim to advance human rights and guarantee their unwavering respect, free from discrimination or infringement. [1]

When defining diplomatic objectives related to human rights, these objectives must stem from a comprehensive and sustainable vision aimed at achieving progress and positive change in the field of human rights. The objectives should be directly relevant to global, regional and local human rights issues and reflect the international community's aspirations for a world characterised by justice and human rights. [2]

Furthermore, it is very important that the objectives are feasible and achievable in partnership with relevant stakeholders, whether international or local, and that they comply with international human rights laws and standards. Setting diplomatic goals related to human rights also requires clarity of vision and a desire to create a positive and tangible impact on the human rights situation, whether through institutional and legal improvements or through changing the behaviours and policies of states and actors. [3]

These objectives must be rooted in a profound understanding of human, social, and political circumstances [4] and take into account local cultures and traditions, as well as the unique challenges of each society and country. In conclusion, setting diplomatic goals related to human rights is a crucial step in the process of promoting human rights through diplomacy. We must ensure that these goals are effectively and sustainably implemented to achieve the desired change and contribute to building a more just and humane world.

Using international platforms to promote human rights issues

International platforms can be effective tools for promoting and highlighting human rights issues in the international community. Diplomats and activists can use international platforms such as the United Nations and international courts to influence human rights developments. Presenting well-researched reports and statements on human rights violations and the necessary corrective measures is the optimal way to employ influence efforts.

International events, such as conferences and summits, can also be used to highlight human rights issues and emphasise the need for collective action to bring about change. Legitimising and gaining international support for human rights movements reinforces the message and makes it possible to put pressure on regimes that violate rights. Thus, it appears that the intelligent and strategic use of international platforms can have a significant impact on achieving reforms and improving human rights in the international arena.

Developing bilateral and multilateral partnerships

Developing bilateral and multilateral partnerships is one of the most important diplomatic strategies that contribute to the promotion of human rights at the international level. The success of diplomacy in promoting human rights depends on its ability to build effective and strong alliances with various stakeholders, whether international or local. Bilateral and multilateral partnerships are based on the idea of joint cooperation to achieve specific goals related to the promotion and protection of human rights. [5]

These partnerships can be between states, international organisations, government institutions, and non-governmental organisations. The development of these partnerships is considered one of the methods of contemporary diplomacy that aims to create a positive and effective impact in the field of human rights. Developing bilateral and multilateral partnerships requires the ability to negotiate and manage diplomatic relations wisely and in positive faith, with an emphasis on the principles of transparency and mutual respect.

Achieving common goals requires close cooperation between the parties involved and finding innovative and sustainable solutions to complex human rights issues. These partnerships must be flexible and able to adapt to changes in international policies and circumstances, which requires prudence and continuity in diplomatic work. The development of bilateral and multilateral partnerships is an essential part of modern and sophisticated diplomacy and represents an effective response to human rights challenges in an era of globalisation and international interdependence.

Negotiation as a tool for improving human rights standards

Negotiation is an effective tool for promoting human rights standards and achieving progress in this area. Diplomatic negotiation on human rights requires high-level communication and conflict management skills, as diplomats seek to reach agreements and decisions that protect and promote human rights. In this context, negotiation is a means of overcoming differences and finding radical solutions to complex human rights issues. One of the most important aspects of negotiation is its ability to broaden participation and collective bargaining on human rights issues. Negotiation can be an effective means of involving different and relevant parties in the formulation of policies and procedures for the protection of human rights. Furthermore, negotiation promotes cooperation and consensus among different parties with a view to strengthening ethical and humanitarian values. The role of negotiation is not limited to reaching agreements and making decisions but also extends to the implementation of those decisions. For example, negotiation can be used to ensure compliance with international human rights standards and accountability in cases of violations. [6]

Thus, negotiation can form an essential part of the diplomatic framework for achieving progress in the field of human rights. Finally, diplomats must be cautious and sensitive in using negotiation as a tool to improve human rights standards, as the focus should be on protecting the vulnerable and contributing to building an international community that respects and promotes human rights for all without discrimination.

Diplomatic action in times of human rights crises

Diplomatic action in times of human rights crises is one of the most important challenges facing human rights diplomats. In such circumstances, immediate and effective decisions and actions are required to protect and promote the human rights at stake. Through decisive and effective diplomatic intervention, support and protection can be provided to those affected, ongoing violations can be stopped, and assurances can be given that they will not be repeated. Diplomatic action in times of human rights crises is based on several fundamental principles, including rapid response and determination to identify immediate solutions, as well as the need to rely on international human rights laws and standards as a basic reference. [7].

Diplomatic actions must be coordinated and integrated with the efforts of the international community and relevant organisations, with a focus on achieving justice and providing the necessary support to victims. [8] The role of diplomacy in such times also includes the direct and personal representation of human rights issues in international forums and conferences, in addition to diplomatic communication and building bridges for dialogue between conflicting parties. The diplomatic role also includes exerting pressure and influence on decision-makers and influential figures to ensure justice and accountability.[9]

Diplomatic moves in times of human rights crises require a great capacity for analysis and an optimal assessment of the situation, while maintaining flexibility and the ability to adapt to rapid developments. Diplomatic plans must be well-thought-out and carefully considered, with a focus on achieving positive and tangible results in a short time. [10] Crisis management and diplomatic action in such situations require a specialised and qualified team capable of dealing with the challenges of the crisis effectively and efficiently.

The role of media and strategic communication in supporting rights

Media and social media play a vital role in promoting and supporting human rights issues at the international level. They are not merely a means of conveying news, but also an effective tool for raising awareness and shaping public opinion on human rights issues. [11] Diplomats and human rights activists should understand the importance of using these tools strategically and intelligently to gain international support and make an effective impact.

The messages conveyed through the media and social media should have a positive impact on public opinion and encourage action and change towards achieving justice and respect for human rights. [12] The media and social media should also be used to monitor human rights violations and document evidence and testimonies that support diplomatic and legal efforts in international communities. [13]

In addition, dialogue and interaction with media and communication platforms are an important part of building effective partnerships with media organisations and the public, which contribute to strengthening support and influence on human rights issues. Despite the importance of the media and social media, efforts must be well-thought-out and coordinated, including careful analysis of expected outcomes and regular evaluation of the strategies used to ensure that they are successful and achieve the desired impact.

Education and training: strengthening diplomatic competencies

The need to strengthen diplomatic competencies in the field of human rights requires significant attention to the role of education and training. Diplomats working in this field need a profound understanding of the principles of human rights and their practical applications at the national and international levels. Hence, the importance and necessity of providing specialised education and training programmes in the field of human rights and diplomacy. [14] These programmes should be comprehensive and multi-level, covering both the theoretical and practical aspects of diplomatic work in support of human rights. [15]

Studies of contemporary issues and historical cases should be included to enhance understanding and develop the necessary skills. We should also provide opportunities for practical training and participation in actual diplomatic processes. [16] Such instruction is essential for building the competencies and negotiation and communication skills needed to deal with human rights issues efficiently and effectively.

To emphasise the importance of this aspect, investments in education and training reflect a serious interest in building a generation of diplomats qualified to deal with human rights challenges and issues in a creative and effective manner. Qualification and training are two fundamental pillars for improving the capabilities of diplomats and equipping them to play an active role in promoting and defending human rights on the international and national stages.

Evaluating Strategies: Criteria for Success and Effectiveness

When developing diplomatic strategies to promote human rights, it is crucial to assess their effectiveness.

Strategy evaluation plays a vital role in understanding whether efforts have achieved their desired goals. Due to the complexities that may surround the field of human rights and diplomacy, evaluation must be comprehensive and thorough. [17]

This requires us to define criteria for success and effectiveness before embarking on a strategy. Criteria for success may include achieving specific goals, such as improving the human rights situation in a particular region or gaining international support for a particular human rights issue. In addition, we must monitor the effectiveness and efficiency of the use of resources, whether financial or human, and determine whether the strategy has contributed to maximising the use of these resources without waste or squandering.

The evaluation should be comprehensive, covering various aspects of the strategy, including an assessment of the social, political, and economic impacts of the efforts made. [18] Furthermore, the evaluation may include a comparative study of the different methods used and an analysis of their respective effectiveness. [19] By analysing the available data and information, we can assess the extent to which the strategy has had a positive impact on human rights. Ultimately, evaluation is not just an analysis of the past, but also a continuous learning process aimed at improving future strategies and increasing their effectiveness in supporting human rights.

Towards innovative and sustainable strategies

Diplomats and decision-makers should be aware that promoting human rights requires persistent and continuous efforts, and that the strategies adopted must be innovative and sustainable to remain effective in the long term. It is essential to think within a framework of justice and fairness to ensure equality and dignity for all human beings without discrimination.

Future strategies must take into account the different cultures and backgrounds of individuals and rely on encouraging cooperation and strengthening partnerships between states, international organisations and civil society. The role of technology and innovation in promoting human rights must also be considered, for example, by leveraging social media and information technology to raise awareness and monitor rights violations. Finally, we must ensure the sustainability of new strategies by periodically evaluating their success and their potential to promote rights and freedoms for everyone.

References

Effective Diplomacy

[1] Srivastava (2021) analysed archival evidence from Amnesty International's early years to highlight how non-governmental organisations engage with governments to achieve human rights goals.
Srivastava, S. "Navigating NGO-Government Relations in Human Rights: New Archival Evidence from Amnesty International, 1961–1986." International Studies Quarterly, 2021.

[2] I. Salama. 'Human Rights Diplomacy From A UN Perspective: A Complement To Advocacy.' (2011): 129–154. https://doi.org/10.1163/ej.9789004195165.i-301.49.

[3] Chinese human rights diplomacy includes the principle of sovereignty in the multilateral arena, dialogue, negotiation, bargaining, and economic incen-

tives in bilateral channels, and tailored and flexible policies on specific issues.

Yuchao Zhu. 'China and International 'Human Rights Diplomacy'.' *China: An International Journal*, 9 (2011): 217–245. https://doi.org/10.1142/S0219747211000148.

[4] Focusing on universal human rights standards and encouraging dialogue among companies can be effective diplomatic methods for promoting human rights, as in Japan.

Ryan Ashley and Elliot Silverberg. 'Japan's Human Rights Diplomacy: A Convergence of Geopolitical and Geoeconomic Interests.' *Asia Policy*, 29 (2022): 125–154. https://doi.org/10.1353/asp.2022.0031.

[5] Altafin et al. (2017) examined the EU's Global Strategy for Foreign and Security Policy and discussed how it aims to develop partnerships and coherence in promoting human rights externally. Altafin, Chiara, Veronika Haász, and Karolina Podstawa. "The New Global Strategy for the EU's Foreign and Security Policy at a Time of Human Rights Crises." Netherlands Quarterly of Human Rights 35 (2017): 122–43.

[6] Human rights diplomacy plays an important role in transforming countries such as South Africa from repressive regimes to ones that respect human rights. See:

Naeli Fitria. "Exploring the Impact of Human Rights on Diplomatic Relations: A Comparative Analysis of State Interactions." COMSERVA: Jurnal Penelitian dan Pengabdian Masyarakat (2023). https://doi.org/10.59141/comserva.v3i1.755.

[7] Bogatyreva (2022) studied humanitarian diplomacy in Latin America, focusing on regional responses to human rights crises and the protection of vulnerable groups.

Bogatyreva, O. "Humanitarian Diplomacy and Human Rights in Latin America. Regional and Civilizational Specifics." Latinskaia Amerika, 2022.

[8] Thuzar (2023) analysed the diplomatic responses of the Association of Southeast Asian Nations to human rights crises in Myanmar, illustrating the regional approach to addressing gross human rights violations.

Thuzar, M. "Myanmar and the Responsibility to Protect: Principles, Precedents, and Practicalities." Journal of International Peacekeeping, 2023.

[9] Zhu, Y. (2011). Cited source.

[10] Anupama Ghosal and Sreeja Pal. (2020): Cited source.

[11] Nike and Dunan (2023) studied the organisational communication climate of the Human Rights Promotion Support Bureau during the COVID-19 pandemic and found that appropriate organisational policies in communication management can stimulate employee productivity.

Nike, De, and Amri Dunan. "Organisational Communication Climate of Human Rights Promotion Support Bureau During Covid-19 Pandemic." Jurnal Spektrum Komunikasi, 2023.

[12] Yustitia et al. (2023) studied how media framing of human rights issues in Indonesia is used to clarify the human rights situation. The study found that hu-

man rights frameworks remained stagnant between 2009 and 2019, with limited ability to mobilise other systems to engage with human rights issues.

Yustitia, Senja, Nunung Prajarto, and Budi Irawanto. "Media Irritability: Exploration of Human Rights Issues in Indonesia During 2009-2019." Jurnal Komunikasi: Malaysian Journal of Communication, 2023.

[13] Jassim (2023) analysed the role of social media in promoting cultural rights, considering that social media contributes significantly to the promotion of cultural rights through openness, interaction and cultural communication between different peoples.

Jassim Raqib Muhammad. 2023. "The Role of Social Media in Promoting Cultural Rights." Al-Kitab Journal for Human Sciences 4 (6):233-56. https://doi.org/10.32441/kjhs.4.6.13.

[14] Koo (2023) analysed the factors influencing school principals' perceptions of human rights through human rights education training, emphasising the need for training to improve skills and flexibility in dealing with human rights issues.

Koo, Jeong-Hwa. 'Analysis of Human Rights Education Training Factors Influencing the Human Rights Perception of Principals.' The Institute for Education and Research Gyeongin National University of Education, 2023.

[15] Soto et al. (2023) examined proposals for training teachers and educational institutions to contribute to the realisation of the human right to education, emphasising the need for a human rights-based

approach to education.

Soto, Idana Beroska Rincon, Betty Janeth Soledispa Cañarte, P. S. Soledispa Cañarte, Julián Steve Guzmán Rodríguez, and Nayibe Soraya Sanchez Leon. "Contribution to the Exercise of the Human Right to Education: Training Proposals for Teachers, Educational Institutions and Teachers." Salud, Ciencia y Tecnología, 2023.

[16] Puhach (2023) conducted a definitive analysis of key concepts in the professional training of future human rights defenders in higher education institutions, highlighting the importance of developing their professional competence.

Puhach, Vitalina. "Definitive Analysis of Key Concepts of the Professional Training of Future Human Rights Defenders in Institutions of Higher Education." Health and Safety Pedagogy, 2023.

[17] Machain (2023) investigated whether US military training is effective in promoting respect for human rights in recipient countries and found that human rights-focused training leads to improvements only in very limited cases.

Machain, C. "School of Influence: Human Rights Challenges in US Foreign Military Training." Conflict Management and Peace Science 41 (2023): 3–25.

[18] Strezhnev et al. (2021) examined claims about the negative spillover effects of human rights promotion efforts, proposed methods for evaluating these arguments, and found weak evidence for the counterclaims in previous studies.

Strezhnev, Anton, J. Kelley, and B. Simmons. "Testing for Negative Spillovers: Is Promoting Human Rights Really Part of the 'Problem'?" International Organization 75 (2021): 71–102.

[19] Luongo (2023) analysed how states use moral disengagement strategies to justify human rights violations, highlighting the need to understand these mechanisms in order to hold states accountable and prevent violations.

Luongo, Ben. "Human Rights Violations, Moral Emotions, and Moral Disengagement: How States Use Moral Disengagement to Justify Their Human Rights Abuses." Journal of Human Rights Practice, 2023.

11
Technology and Human Rights
Future Opportunities for Advancing Rights

The Relationship Between Technology and Human Rights

The relationship between technology and human rights is a fascinating topic that deserves deep reflection and ongoing discussion. Today, we are on the cusp of a massive digital revolution that is radically transforming how humans interact with technology and how it affects our lives and rights. The relationship between technology and human rights dates back to ancient times, when technological innovations influenced people's ability to exercise their rights and freedoms. In the Middle Ages, a revolution in agricultural and industrial technologies flourished, leading to a significant change in the structure of society and, consequently, a profound impact on human rights and how they were exercised.

On the other hand, the Fourth Industrial Revolution, or what is known as the digital industrial revolution, has brought about tremendous shifts in technology's ability to absorb and analyse vast amounts of data quickly and accurately. This shift raises many questions about how these advanced technologies affect human rights and whether they may lead to the promotion or restriction of these rights. [1]

A review of the basic theories linking technology and human rights reveals many different trends and philosophical schools of thought that attempt to understand this complex relationship. By studying these theories and historical developments, we can paint a comprehensive picture of this relationship and identify the challenges and opportunities it presents.

The digital revolution and its impact on human rights

In our current era, we are witnessing a tremendous digital revolution in various aspects of life, and we have noticed the effects of this revolution on the lives of individuals and societies in ways that were not previously expected. Digital technology has fundamentally transformed the way humans engage with their surroundings and each other. These developments have brought with them both challenges and opportunities in the field of human rights. From this perspective, it is important to study the impact of the digital revolution on human rights in a detailed and comprehensive manner. [2]

The impact of the digital revolution extends to a wide range of human rights issues. We can first look at privacy rights and personal freedoms. Digital technology has brought with it significant challenges in terms of protecting individuals' data and maintaining the confidentiality of their personal information. [3] We must examine how technology can be used to preserve individuals' privacy and enhance the protection of their rights in this context. [4] In addition, we can also discuss how technology can be used to support human rights and combat injustice and oppression.

For example, social media and the internet can be used to raise awareness about human rights issues and document violations, thereby increasing international pressure to stop them. Technology can also empower marginalised groups, empowering them to participate in decision-making and assert their rights. It is therefore important to explore in detail how human rights can be promoted through the optimal use of digital technology, as well as how to address the challenges that this technology poses to fundamental human rights.

Modern technological tools for monitoring and enforcing human rights

Modern technology has led to the emergence of numerous technological tools for monitoring and enforcing human rights. Research and reports indicate that these tools have both positive and negative aspects, and require careful assessment of their impact on society and human rights. [5] These technological tools include online surveillance and monitoring systems, automatic facial recognition, big data analysis, and others.

The increasing prevalence of online surveillance and monitoring systems may contribute to improving public security, but it may also pose a threat to the individual rights of citizens. Should privacy rights be sacrificed in exchange for security? [6] This question requires comprehensive and objective discussion. Automatic facial recognition can improve security and confirm identity, but it also brings up concerns about privacy and discrimination.

In addition, big data analysis can contribute to a more profound understanding of the needs and challenges facing communities, but caution must be exercised to prevent misuse and violation of individual privacy. Decision-makers and the international community must work together to develop a regulatory framework and laws that ensure the responsible use of these tools and protect human rights. History demonstrates that technology is merely a tool, and its ultimate influence hinges on its application. Therefore, we must strive to direct technology to serve the promotion of rights and freedoms in communities around the world.

Artificial intelligence and its role in supporting human rights issues

Developments in artificial intelligence are one of the most influential areas of our lives in the 21st century, and these influences are beginning to emerge in the context of human rights issues. [7] Artificial intelligence is an effective tool in supporting and promoting human rights in various ways. [8] Artificial intelligence can be used to detect human rights violations by analysing and understanding big data to identify patterns of violations and direct efforts towards preventing them. [9]

Furthermore, artificial intelligence technologies can be used to develop early warning systems to predict rights violations and take appropriate action. It is worth noting that AI can also be a fundamental pillar in achieving social solidarity and justice, as it can be used to analyse data to guide public policies and social programmes towards groups in need. [10]

However, it is important to warn of the challenges that may arise from the use of artificial intelligence for human rights issues, such as privacy and the negative use of technologies for control and repression. Efforts should be directed towards developing a strict legal and ethical framework that regulates the use of artificial intelligence in the context of human rights and ensures that technology is for the benefit of humanity in general.

Data privacy challenges in the information age

In the modern information age, we face significant challenges related to data privacy. Data has become an essential part of individuals and organisations' lives, and we must be extremely cautious about how it is collected and used. [11] Personal data must be strictly and effectively protected to ensure its privacy and integrity.

One of the major challenges is the increasing scope of data collection and use without the explicit consent of individuals. These situations can lead to a breach of privacy and trust between individuals and organisations. Data leaks and cyber breaches are also among the most serious threats to data privacy in the digital age.

Such incidents can lead to the unlawful exploitation of personal data and cause significant harm to individuals and organisations. Furthermore, the growth of facial recognition and electronic tracking technologies may lead to the violation of individuals' privacy and undermine the right to private life. These challenges require strict measures to protect data privacy, including effective legal legislation and strict regulatory systems. [12]

It is also necessary to educate individuals about the importance of protecting their personal data and raise their awareness of the potential risks. Companies and governments should be responsible for implementing strict security and privacy measures to protect data. Striking a balance between using data to achieve technological advancement and ensuring privacy protection is a major challenge that requires a comprehensive vision and joint efforts from all parties concerned.

The Internet is a space for freedom and the exchange of ideas

The Internet is an important key to promoting freedom of expression and the exchange of ideas in our societies today. It provides a means for individuals to communicate and interact regardless of geographical or cultural boundaries. Through the internet, individuals can express their views and opinions almost freely and without restriction, promoting intellectual diversity and virtual democracy. Through social media platforms and personal blogs, individuals can contribute to public dialogue and discussions on politics and culture, as well as share experiences and knowledge.

However, alongside these benefits, challenges concerning human rights and the freedom of expression on the internet have also arisen.[13] Many countries experience internet restrictions and strict government censorship, which can lead to the suppression of freedom of expression and the narrowing of virtual space. It is not only the role of governments; technology companies also face challenges around privacy and content control. [14]

Therefore, it is important to educate people about their digital rights and promote dialogue on the importance of protecting freedom of expression and privacy online. In this way, the internet can remain an open space for freedom, expression and the exchange of ideas, contributing to the promotion of human rights and the building of more interactive and empathetic societies.

Technology and the promotion of marginalised groups' rights

Modern technology provides powerful tools for promoting the rights of marginalised groups in society. Through technology, access to basic services, such as education, healthcare, and employment opportunities, can be expanded for people with special needs and poor communities. Technology can be used to provide platforms for distance learning and free educational resources for all, helping to reduce the educational gap between different classes in society. In addition, technology can be used to develop innovative solutions to societal problems such as food and water shortages and to improve living conditions in remote areas.

Economically, technology can contribute to promoting employment opportunities for marginalised groups by creating new jobs in the fields of technology and innovation. [15] However, we must be cautious about the emergence of new digital divides that may exacerbate inequalities in access to technology and its benefits among social classes. [16]

There is an urgent need to ensure that information and communication technology is inclusive and accessible to all, without discrimination or bias. We must also ensure that artificial intelligence and facial recognition technologies do not contribute to discrimination and human rights violations against marginalised groups. Policies on the use of technology must be geared towards promoting equality, justice and social sustainability. Ultimately, information and communication technology can be a positive force in supporting the rights of marginalised groups if used correctly and responsibly. Policymakers and decision-makers must commit to ensuring that this technology serves the interests of all without exception and promotes justice and human rights for all.

Robots and human rights: ethical and legal challenges

Advanced technology and the use of artificial intelligence in robotics are among the most significant technological developments that may pose new ethical and legal challenges to human rights. In this context, the use of robots in areas such as healthcare and industrial work raises important questions about safety, security and the protection of human rights. [17]

We must view robots not only as advanced machines but also as an ethical and legal proposition. What are the rights of robots, and what about their responsibilities? Should robots be bound by laws that guarantee the protection of fundamental rights and human dignity? On the other hand, the use of robots in society raises ethical challenges regarding the question of responsibility and social sensitivity. [18]

Given the decisions that robots can make, should we be concerned about their impact on human lives and rights? How can we ensure that interactions between humans and robots are based on values of justice and rights? With these challenges in mind, we need to develop a legal and ethical framework that ensures adequate protection of human rights in the face of technological advances. Reflection on robots and their applications requires a broad and comprehensive discussion involving experts in law, ethics and technology to develop policies and guidelines that promote the use of robots in a way that balances technological progress and human rights.

Examples of using technology to protect rights

Information and communication technology (ICT) is a powerful tool for promoting and protecting human rights around the world, and there are many examples of how this technology can be used to support fundamental human rights principles. Artificial intelligence technologies, for instance, can monitor and analyse health data in medical and health applications to enhance treatment and healthcare outcomes. In the area of protecting freedom of expression, social media provides opportunities for individuals to express their opinions and organise in favour of their rights and freedoms.

In addition, there are technological applications that offer effective models for monitoring human rights and addressing persecution and violations. For example, the widespread use of surveillance cameras and tracking technologies in humanitarian operations can greatly contribute to gathering evidence and monitoring violations. In the legal context, technology provides tools to enhance access to justice and enable individuals to file complaints and legal documents in simple and effective ways. These global models reflect the enormous opportunities that technology offers in the field of rights protection and the positive transformations it can bring about in dealing with human rights issues around the world.

Future steps for integrating technology with human rights

With the spread of technology and its continuous development, there is a need to develop future plans for integrating these technologies into the support and protection of human rights. We must first consider how to leverage modern technology in developing mechanisms used to monitor and evaluate human rights. Big data analytics and artificial intelligence technologies can be used to better understand trends and patterns associated with human rights violations and to build effective strategies to address them. In addition, geographic information systems and remote sensing technologies can be integrated to monitor areas where violations are likely to occur and intervene in a timely manner to prevent them.

However, we must be cautious and acknowledge that there are potential risks associated with this use, such as privacy violations and data misuse. On the other hand, it is also important to highlight the role of technology in promoting communication and disseminating knowledge about human rights. Social media and various digital platforms can be used as tools to educate people about their rights and raise awareness of the importance of respecting human rights and reducing violations. Furthermore, we can develop mobile applications and interactive platforms that offer easily accessible information and resources related to human rights.

Furthermore, future steps also need to focus on a legal framework that ensures the protection of privacy and personal data in the context of the integration of technology into human rights. Laws and policies should be developed that define the permissible use of data and establish strict controls to prevent misuse and privacy violations.

In addition, effective oversight and monitoring mechanisms should be established to monitor the use of technology and ensure that it is used in accordance with human rights principles. Ultimately, we must recognise that the integration of technology into human rights requires a balance between exploiting the potential benefits of this technology to protect rights and address violations and addressing the potential challenges and risks associated with it. Future steps must therefore be based on ethics and fundamental human rights principles to ensure that technology is used responsibly and effectively in support of human rights.

References

Technology and Human Rights

[1] Kanetake (2018) examined the European Union's export controls on electronic surveillance technology and their implications for human rights approaches.
Kanetake, M. "The EU's Export Control of Cyber Surveillance Technology: Human Rights Approaches." Business and Human Rights Journal, 2018.

[2] Heller (2023) explored how immersive technologies such as virtual reality and augmented reality are reshaping human rights considerations.
Heller, Brittan. "Reimagining Reality: Human Rights and Immersive Technology." Social Science Research Network, 2023.

[3] Shehu and Shehu (2023) analyse data rights protection in the age of technology, exploring the intersection of human rights and data rights in the digital

age.

Shehu, Vlona Pollozhani, and Visar Shehu. "Human Rights in the Technology Era – Protection of Data Rights." European Journal of Economics, Law and Social Sciences 7 (2023): 1–10.

[4] Kathuria et al. (2023) examined the creation of human rights in technology through artificial intelligence, proposing a methodology for incorporating human rights protection into digital technologies.

Kathuria, Samta, Poonam Rawat, Rajesh Singh, Anita Gehlot, Namrata Kathuria, and Shweta Pandey. "Artificial Intelligence: Creation of Human Rights in Technology." In Artificial Intelligence and Symbolic Computation, 328–31, 2023.

[5] Whitty (2010) examined how soldier photography and digital technology influenced human rights documentation in the context of the abuse of detainees in Iraq.

Whitty, N. "Soldier Photography of Detainee Abuse in Iraq: Digital Technology, Human Rights and the Death of Baha Mousa." Human Rights Law Review 10 (2010): 689–714.

[6] Humphreys, S. "Navigating the Dataverse: Privacy, Technology, Human Rights," 2011.

[7] Gregory (2023) discussed strategies for defending human rights in an age of deepfakes and generative AI, focusing on how to "fortify the truth" in digital environments.

Gregory, Sam. "Fortify the Truth: How to Defend Human Rights in an Age of Deepfakes and Generative

AI." Journal of Human Rights Practice, 2023.

[8] Land, Molly K., and J. D. Aronson. "Human Rights and Technology: New Challenges for Justice and Accountability." Annual Review of Law and Social Science, 2020.

[9] Fernández-Aller et al. (2021) proposed a comprehensive and sustainable AI strategy for Europe based on human rights principles.

Fernández-Aller, Celia, Arturo Fernández Velasco, Ángeles Manjarrés, D. Pastor-Escuredo, S. Pickin, Jesús Salgado Criado, and T. Ausín. "An Inclusive and Sustainable Artificial Intelligence Strategy for Europe Based on Human Rights." IEEE Technology & Society Magazine 40 (2021): 46–54.

[10] Soh and Connolly (2020) explored how the Fourth Industrial Revolution, including artificial intelligence, is impacting business and human rights, defining new frontiers of profit and risk.

Soh, Changrok, and Daniel Connolly. "New Frontiers of Profit and Risk: The Fourth Industrial Revolution's Impact on Business and Human Rights." New Political Economy 26 (2020): 168–85.

[11] Sekalala et al. (2020) analysed the impact of increased digital surveillance of public health on human rights during the COVID-19 crisis, examining the challenges to privacy rights posed by new surveillance technologies.

Sekalala, S., Stéphanie Dagron, L. Forman, and B. Meier. "Analysing the Human Rights Impact of Increased Digital Public Health Surveillance during the

COVID-19 Crisis." Health and Human Rights: An International Journal 22 (2020): 7–20.

[12] Bwana (2024) examined Kenya's digital identity revolution, analysing the balance between technological progress and human rights, including data privacy challenges.

Bwana, Ronald Odhiambo. "Kenya's Digital Identity Revolution: Balancing Progress and Human Rights." Global Privacy Law Review, 2024.

[13] Gregory (2023) discussed strategies for defending human rights in an age of deepfakes and generative AI, focusing on how to "fortify the truth" in digital environments.

Gregory, Sam. "Fortify the Truth: How to Defend Human Rights in an Age of Deepfakes and Generative AI." Journal of Human Rights Practice, 2023.

[14] Burri (2023) examined the intersection of digital trade law and human rights, including the implications for freedom of expression online.

Burri, Mira. "Digital Trade Law and Human Rights." AJIL Unbound 117 (2023): 110–15.

[15] Nnamdi et al. (2023) assessed the impact of artificial intelligence on social and economic human rights, focusing on automation and job loss, which can disproportionately affect marginalised groups.

Nnamdi, Nmesoma, Babafemi Zacchaeus Ogunlade, and B. Abegunde. "An Evaluation of the Impact of Artificial Intelligence on Socio-Economic Human Rights: A Discourse on Automation and Job Loss." Scholars International Journal of Law Crime and Justice, 2023.

[16] Molnár (2019) examined artificial intelligence and global migration management from a human rights perspective, discussing how technology affects marginalised migrant populations.

Molnár, P. "Technology on the Margins: AI and Global Migration Management from a Human Rights Perspective." Springer International Publishing 8 (2019): 305–30.

[17] Chyhryna, Halyna. "Permissibility of Using Artificial Intelligence in Law Enforcement Activities." Actual Problems of Innovative Economy and Law, 2024.

[18] Kruby and Shenin (2023) analysed how the Convention rights of persons with disabilities applies to decision-making processes in the field of artificial intelligence, addressing the ethical and legal challenges posed by artificial intelligence and robotics.

Krupiy, T., and M. Scheinin. "Disability Discrimination in the Digital Realm: How the ICRPD Applies to Artificial Intelligence Decision-Making Processes and Helps in Determining the State of International Human Rights Law." Human Rights Law Review, 2023.

12
Conclusion
Towards Diplomacy Based on Awareness and Responsibility

A Review of Diplomacy and Human Rights

Reviewing the historical development of diplomacy and human rights is essential to understanding the context in which we find ourselves today.

Diplomacy began as a concept in ancient times, when kingdoms sent envoys to negotiate with other kingdoms and resolve disputes. It can be said that the first real diplomatic exchange took place during the monarchy, when state institutions were used to regulate relations with neighbours and strangers. The concept of human rights dates back to the early periods of human history and was represented by attempts to set limits on the power of government and protect individuals from abuse and injustice. As times evolved and expanded, diplomacy underwent radical transformations, becoming more professional and complex, based on in-depth rules. In this context, the concepts of human rights have evolved to include a wide range of rights and freedoms that individuals should enjoy as part of their humanity.

Providing means of protection and guarantees for these rights has become vital and necessary for diplomacy to play an active role in preserving human dignity and ensuring the stability of societies. The evolution of diplomacy and human rights plays a crucial role in the course of human history and highlights how social and political circumstances influence these concepts. By understanding this evolution, we can envision future trends in diplomacy and human rights and entrust the new generation with the responsibility of building on these experiences and knowledge.

Lessons from history and their contemporary applications

Studying diplomatic history and the evolution of human rights throughout the ages provides valuable lessons that can help us understand current challenges and build more effective diplomacy. By analysing experiences, we can draw many useful lessons and apply them in the current context. History shows how the dynamics of diplomacy have changed over time and how they have been influenced by political, social and technological developments.

One of the most important lessons we can learn is the growing recognition of the need to integrate human rights into all diplomatic activities. From this, we can understand the importance of recognising the human dimensions of policymaking and decision-making. History also shows us how international solidarity and mutual cooperation can lead to the improvement of human rights and the promotion of the common good.

Furthermore, studying history can show us the mistakes made in the field of human rights diplomacy in the past and how they can be avoided in the future. Analysing history can also point to successful diplomatic models that can serve as examples for transformations in modern diplomacy. In the current context, diplomacy must be based on awareness and responsibility, which we can achieve by drawing lessons from history and applying them to current challenges. These lessons and applications are key to building a more humane and just world.

Key challenges facing human rights diplomacy

In the context of contemporary developments, human rights diplomacy faces many challenges that require deep reflection and comprehensive preparation. One of the most prominent challenges is the increase in political and cultural divisions in global societies, which affects the ability of diplomats to reach international agreements that promote human rights. Furthermore, the current era has seen an increase in security and terrorist challenges, making it difficult for diplomats to strike a balance between maintaining security and ensuring respect for human rights.

In this context, diplomats must seek comprehensive and balanced solutions to overcome these security and political challenges in ways that ensure a clear diplomatic vision that promotes human rights. On the other hand, there is the challenge of the rapid pace of technological change and its impact on human rights. Modern technology opens new doors to privacy violations and security threats that require an effective diplomatic response.

Nevertheless, diplomats must work to exploit the opportunities offered by technology to promote human rights, transparency and accountability. The economic and social challenges that affect the stability of human rights cannot be ignored and require diplomatic solutions that take economic and social aspects into account. By carefully studying these challenges, diplomats can develop integrated strategies to address the challenges of promoting human rights in the modern era.

The Relationship Between Technology and the Promotion of Human Rights

Technology is an integral part of our daily lives and has brought about radical transformations in all areas of life, including human rights. While it has provided opportunities to support human rights through technology, it has also created new challenges and issues that need to be considered and addressed. One of the effects of technology on human rights is that it provides greater access to information and communication, enabling individuals to express their opinions and demand their rights more through social media and other digital platforms. However, we must be cautious, as technology can increase inequality and promote human rights violations if not used properly.

Technology has evolved in multiple directions, including artificial intelligence, optical analysis, data tracking, and encryption, opening the door to new and innovative uses for promoting and protecting human rights. However, we must also recognise the potential challenges associated with technology, such as cyber-attacks, data espionage, and privacy violations, which can negatively impact human rights. This requires a profound understanding of technology and the ability to keep pace with developments and understand their potential impact on human rights.

Diplomats and decision-makers should also take responsibility for shaping regulatory and legislative policies that ensure technology is used to promote and protect human rights without compromising fundamental freedoms and privacy. Hence, the importance of adopting a comprehensive and balanced approach that combines technology and human rights to achieve sustainable and inclusive development in societies.

The role of awareness and education in building responsible diplomacy

Awareness and education play a prominent role in building responsible diplomacy towards human rights. The world faces serious challenges in the field of human rights resulting from a lack of awareness and education on these issues and their impact at the diplomatic level. Community awareness plays a crucial role in supporting and strengthening diplomatic efforts aimed at human rights.

Awareness of the importance of human rights and the need to respect them must be promoted through education and awareness-raising, both in schools and in social and media circles. Similarly, effective education can equip young people with the values and knowledge that will enable them to adopt informed and effective diplomatic positions on human rights issues.

The international community should intensify its efforts to develop and implement awareness-raising and educational programmes targeting different segments of society, with the aim of increasing awareness of the importance of human rights and the role of diplomacy in promoting them. We should also create opportunities for the exchange of experiences and ideas between different countries and communities, with the aim of strengthening international cooperation in this field and building responsible diplomacy that seeks to promote human rights at the national and global levels.

The importance of international cooperation in establishing human rights standards

International cooperation is one of the fundamental and necessary pillars for establishing human rights standards at the global level. Through cooperation and coordination between countries, radical changes can be achieved in the protection and promotion of human rights. Countries must work together to develop strong international standards that preserve and support human rights everywhere. Mutual support between countries and cooperation in developing human rights policies and programmes is one effective way to ensure progress in this area.

Furthermore, international cooperation can contribute to raising awareness and education about human rights, thereby promoting universal commitment to these rights. States must also continue to cooperate by providing support and assistance to countries and communities facing challenges in realising human rights through humanitarian, development, and educational programs.

International cooperation is needed to address global challenges that threaten human rights, such as poverty, armed conflict, forced displacement and climate change. Only through comprehensive and genuine cooperation between states can sustainable solutions be reached that achieve respect for and promotion of human rights for all, without exception.

Strategies for gaining public and political support for human rights

Among the vital elements in promoting and consolidating human rights in society is the strategy of gaining public and political support. The positive influence that public opinion and political forces can have on supporting these rights can make a significant difference in achieving progress. This topic deserves careful scrutiny and deep reflection, as successful diplomacy in this regard depends on well-thought-out methods and strategies. It is important to recognise the importance of building alliances with influential political forces in different societies.

Therefore, studying and understanding the trends, priorities and interests related to human rights is essential for identifying opportunities and defining strategic plans. It is also necessary to present a convincing vision and try to build strong arguments that clarify the real benefits of supporting human rights and establishing them in political and social ideologies. This can help to attract public and political support and motivate supportive forces to take effective action. Effective and clear communication with all stakeholders also contributes to building a common understanding and achieving consensus on shared goals.

Efforts must also be directed towards building the capacity of political and public forces to understand, support and realise human rights. To achieve these goals, training, awareness-raising and financial support are urgently needed. Furthermore, clear and reliable data, evidence and reports must be provided to highlight the shortcomings and challenges facing the promotion of human rights and to motivate states and institutions to adopt effective policies and measures to address these issues. Ultimately, it is essential to encourage community participation and raise awareness of the importance of public and political support and commitment to human rights, as this sustained support is the key to achieving lasting positive change.

Analysing effective diplomatic models and developing a forward-looking perspective

Given the evolution of international conditions and the increasing complexity of human rights issues, diplomats must comprehensively analyse effective diplomatic models and highlight their future prospects. The challenges facing the international community require diplomats to develop new strategies in line with changes in the modern world. Diplomatic analysis must be based on a careful study of the various models that can be useful in achieving human rights goals. One important model of effective diplomacy is cultural diplomacy, which focuses on connecting values and civilisations to achieve understanding and cooperation between peoples. The details of this model must be studied, lessons learnt from its experiences must be drawn, and they must be applied in reality.

Economic diplomacy should also be analysed, and an assessment made of how human rights can benefit from trade and economic cooperation between countries. Environmental diplomacy is also an important model to monitor and analyse its impact on human rights, especially in light of growing environmental challenges. In addition, digital diplomacy must be examined, and its effectiveness in achieving humanitarian goals in the age of information technology must be ensured. A forward-looking perspective on these models must also be provided by looking ahead and emerging trends in the complex world of diplomacy.

Diplomatic analysis must be geared towards emerging challenges, such as the impact of economic, social and environmental transformations on human rights. In general, this future analysis should include the implications of technological progress and its social and political impacts on the field of diplomatic work. Focusing on the future helps with strategic planning and provides diplomats with the tools and techniques necessary to deal with future circumstances.

Diplomatic priorities for the coming decades

Our era requires advanced strategic thinking about the role of diplomacy in promoting and protecting human rights in the coming decades. Establishing fundamental human rights principles requires clear and specific priorities that are reflected in diplomatic policies and actions. Among these priorities, issues of diversity and inclusivity must be given high importance. Diplomacy should work to promote equality and combat discrimination in all its forms, both within and between states, through awareness-raising and the development of appropriate policies. Significant attention should also be paid to environmental and development issues, which have become of paramount importance in light of global environmental and economic challenges.

Diplomacy must support efforts to manage natural resources sustainably and address the challenges posed by climate change and environmental degradation. In addition, strategies should also be developed to address economic and social challenges that affect human rights, such as poverty and social marginalisation. It is also necessary to focus on promoting individual freedoms and community participation so that these fundamental priorities of diplomacy are represented in the coming decades.

Diplomacy should also work to promote dialogue between cultures and religions and to foster values of mutual respect and cross-border understanding. Diplomatic action requires comprehensively and holistically addressing the multiple and changing challenges of the 21st century and presenting an integrated vision for promoting human rights and achieving comprehensive and sustainable peace.

Creating a new vision: towards sustainability and inclusivity in human rights diplomacy

Achieving sustainability and inclusivity in human rights diplomacy requires serious steps towards changing mindsets and practices. This new vision must be based on a deep understanding of the contemporary challenges facing human rights and a commitment to the comprehensive application of human rights standards and principles. Human rights diplomats must strive to build international cooperation and partnerships on a solid foundation of trust and mutual respect, with a focus on sustainability and ensuring the full participation of all groups in policy formulation and decision-making.

Promoting the sustainability and inclusiveness of human rights requires directing efforts towards achieving sustainable development that guarantees social justice and basic services for all individuals without discrimination. The role of civil society and democratic institutions in this area should also be activated, including by promoting transparency and accountability and strengthening dialogue between citizens and governments.

Emphasis should also be placed on promoting equality and combating discrimination in all aspects of social and legal life. Achieving this new vision for the future is a challenge for everyone and requires joint efforts and comprehensive commitment from all political and social actors. By creating a new vision for human rights diplomacy, we can build a more just and humane world, where everyone's rights and freedoms are guaranteed without exception.

www.ingramcontent.com/pod-product-compliance
Lightning Source LLC
Chambersburg PA
CBHW051538020426
42333CB00016B/1981